Beyond
Bok
Choy

Beyond Bok Choy

 Rosa Lo San Ross

Photographs by Martin Jacobs

Artisan New York

A COOK'S GUIDE TO ASIAN VEGETABLES

For my mother, Edris de Carvalho,
with love and remembrance

Editor: Ann ffolliott
Production director: Hope Koturo

Published in 1996 by Artisan,
a division of Workman Publishing Company, Inc.
708 Broadway, New York, NY 10003-9555

Library of Congress Cataloging-in-Publication Data
Ross, Rosa Lo San.
Beyond bok choy : a cook's guide to Asian
vegetables, with 70 recipes / by Rosa Lo San Ross :
photographs by Martin Jacobs.
Includes bibliographic references and index.
ISBN 1-885183-23-2
1 Cookery (Vegetables) 2 Cookery, Oriental. I Title
TX801.R7954 1966
641.6'5 — dc20   95-47566

Printed in Italy
10 9 8 7 6 5 4 3 2 1
First Printing

CONTENTS

Introduction

Years ago, when I first left Hong Kong to live in Europe, I was struck by the scarcity of leafy green vegetables during the cold winter months. I longed for the many different varieties found in Hong Kong markets. Later, when I moved to New York, I was delighted to find all my beloved greens in Chinatown, many of them available throughout the year. Today, interest in Asian vegetables has mushroomed. You can walk into almost any North American supermarket and find a large array of Asian vegetables. Farmers markets also offer increasing numbers of them.

Chefs everywhere are using Asian vegetables — in exotic cross-cultural dishes, in classic Asian preparations, and as vegetable side dishes and garnishes. Despite all this, however, there is little specific information available to help cooks identify the fine points of different Asian vegetables and herbs and to explain how to use them. Even Asian recipe books seldom help in this regard.

When I go to Chinatown with my students and friends, I am struck by the fact that, while everyone finds these vegetables intriguing, most are at a loss when it comes to cooking them. At supermarkets, I often notice shoppers indecisively fingering tempting green heads of bok choy and wondering how to prepare them. Recently, I was delighted to find a beautiful bunch of mizuna at my local Long Island supermarket, but even the produce manager didn't know what it was or how to prepare it.

I have tried to include all the vegetables you may see on a visit to Chinatown or an Asian market. In addition to the popular leafy greens, you will also find gourds, melons, squashes, roots, rhizomes, corms, tubers, sprouts, shoots, beans, and the most popular and readily available Chinese and Southeast Asian herbs. Accompaning the recipes are hints on how to buy and store the vegetables, as well as general cooking instructions, so you can be creative and use them in your own ways.

When I first began to develop the recipes, I worried that I would end up with a long list of Asian soups and stir-fries. In fact, you will find recipes that can be considered American, albeit with an Asian accent. Although not a vegetarian book, some recipes are meatless and others can be modified. Many recipes are easy and quick and work well for everyday meals; some are even low in fat. I have included a few recipes — such as one for a tomato coulis — that use western vegetables, because they work well with Asian flavors. This is part of the Chinese way: quickly adopting what is good and fresh. Modern-day Chinese cooking frequently employs shallots, garlic, sweet peppers, leeks, asparagus, cucumbers, carrots, and headed broccoli, all originally from Europe or South or North America. In North American markets, one cannot find true Chinese lettuce, because the Chinese have enthusiastically adopted romaine, Boston, and iceberg.

Some recipes are cross-cultural and some are elegant enough for special occasions. Serving my Scallop Mousse in Bok Choy Packets on a plate glazed with Roasted Tomato Coulis (page 16) would make any cook proud, and the Tamarind-Braised Lamb Shanks (page 184) served with Shiso Risotto (page 177) is easy to make, but rich tasting and exotically different. There are also recipes for sweet and savory sauces, a number of desserts, and even a jam made with vegetables. So you can incorporate Asian vegetables into any part of a meal.

In the 1800s, most of the first Chinese immigrants to this country came from southern China. It is, therefore, understandable that the common transliterated names for most of the "older" Asian vegetables — particularly those available in supermarkets — are in Cantonese. In my years of teaching, I have found it is very difficult to identify a vegetable without actually having the vegetable at hand. So many have similar sounding names, and even in China, the name can vary from one place to another.

In an effort to identify each vegetable as precisely as possible, I have used an English name (sometimes a translation or a transliteration), a Cantonese name, and a botanical name. Of course, the color illustrations will clear up any doubts that may still remain.

Leafy Greens

I thought it appropriate to begin this book with leafy greens, because these are the Asian vegetables with which North Americans are most familiar. Most of these leafy green vegetables are brassicas, either of the cabbage family or the mustard cabbage family. So, while you will find specific recipes for Bok Choy, Flowering Cabbage (*choy sum*), Chinese Broccoli (*gai lan*), and so on, remember that in many instances you can use the brassicas interchangeably. It is always better to use the freshest seasonal vegetable available than to buy the exact one listed in a recipe if it is not in good condition. Don't hesitate to do this when appropriate.

Gourds, Melons & Squashes

The Chinese, particularly the Cantonese, love gourds, melons, and squashes. A light soup made with squash is served at practically every meal, especially during the summer. These soups are very refreshing in hot weather and they are quick and easy to make.

The all-encompassing Chinese word *qwa* is used for all the vegetables in this chapter, even though in English some of them are called gourds, some are squashes, and some are melons. Except for papaya and eggplant, botanically they are all cucurbits.

Although the Chinese love sweet melons such as watermelon, cantaloupe, and honeydew, in this book I am concerned with those most often used in savory dishes. Many Asian melons, however, have an almost neutral flavor and can be used in either savory or sweet dishes. Often, particularly at Chinese New Year, you will find candied pieces of different melons. And, I've included a recipe for Winter Squash Pudding that makes a great dessert.

Roots, Rhizomes, Corms & Tubers

In China, water is so much a part of the cultivation of the land that many vegetables are grown in, around, or under water. The Chinese system of irrigation involves the flooding of land for rice paddies. Ponds dot the landscape and are appreciated as much for their beauty as for providing a fertile place to cultivate fish and aquatic plants. Rivers and canals have historically served as highways for the transport of people and goods, and their banks supply fish, fowl, and plant life for the kitchen.

Many Chinese vegetables — such as Water Chestnuts, Lotus Roots, and Arrowhead Tubers — are the roots of water plants. Cultivation of these plants is not practical for home gardeners, because they require swampy sites, lots of water, and tropical or semi-tropical conditions, but they can easily be found in Asian markets.

A few of these root vegetables — daikon, sweet potato, kohlrabi — are quite common in the west. I have included them because they have been enthusiastically adopted by many Asian cuisines.

Ginger is neither a water plant nor a root; it is a rhizome (the underground stem of the plant, which grows sideways with roots of its own). Chinese food without fresh ginger just won't do, and it has been prized since ancient times for its medicinal and spiritual properties and was found in the famous Han tomb excavated in 1972, buried with a noble lady of twenty-one centuries ago.

Sprouts, Shoots & Beans

A few Asian vegetables are so familiar they seem like old friends. Beansprouts, especially, may have been part of your introduction to Chinese food. They are the one vegetable we can count on finding in any supermarket — if only in cans.

Another old standby is bamboo shoots. Everyone interested in Asian food has tasted bamboo shoots, but I am sure there are quite a few readers who may never have tasted fresh bamboo shoots. If you see them in an Asian market, you will be able to buy and cook them with complete confidence.

Herbs

Herbs are essential ingredients if you want to cook dishes with authentic flavors. I have included the Asian herbs you will find in North America.

These herbs lend themselves to creative uses in cross-cultural dishes. Once you are comfortable using them in native dishes, let your imagination go. The unusual and sometimes exotic flavors will turn an eveyday dish into something special.

Many of these herbs are important to more than one cuisine, but a few are used exclusively in Japanese or Thai cooking. And herbs commonly found in one nation's kitchen may have only a medicinal role in another country. Of course, Asians also use many of the everyday seasonings that are used in other cuisines, such as garlic, shallots, and chili peppers. These are so familiar to everyone that I did not include them in this book.

While researching this book, I found that many seed catalogues carry Asian vegetable seeds — even for some items that are hard to find in Asian markets (see Seed Sources, page 187). Many of these vegetables are easy to grow in your home garden, including most of the popular Asian leafy greens. While this is not a book about growing Asian vegetables, I have included growing hints for those that are easy to cultivate. Try growing one or two new varieties and you will be richly rewarded. There is something deeply satisfying in serving food that you have grown yourself to people you love.

I hope you will read about Asian vegetables, buy them, grow them, cook them, and eat them. I know that these vegetables — like spinach, broccoli, peas, lettuce, carrots, and celery — will become reliable old friends that can be used in your own favorite dishes.

Leafy
Greens

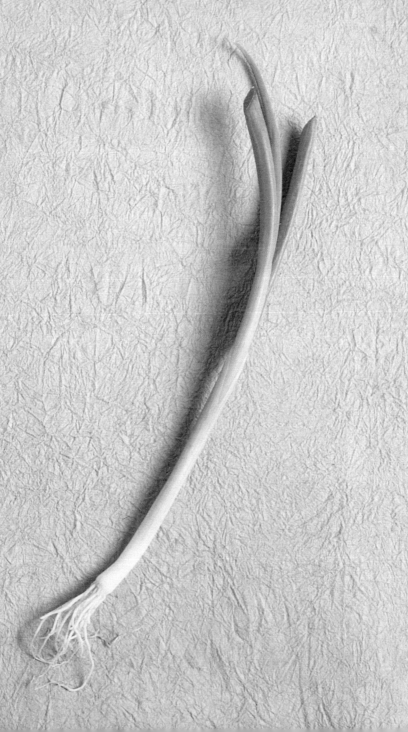

Bok Choy
Bok Choy · Bai Cai
Brassica rapa, Chinensis group

白菜

Whenever I am in Chinatown and I pass the vegetable stalls piled high with bunches of bok choy, with ivory-white stems and bright green leaves, I am reminded of the healthy green vegetables we ate at every meal when I was a child in Hong Kong. We had to eat the greens or answer to our amah, or nanny, who supervised our meals and was a much stricter disciplinarian than our mother. If the vegetable was bok choy, there was never much resistance from me. I loved the tender stems and sweet, sharp flavor, especially when they were simply flavored with ginger and served in a clear broth. To me, bok choy, with its bright green leaves, has always been the perfect "healthy" vegetable, and I am delighted to find mounds of crisp white and green bok choy in so many markets today.

One of the oldest Chinese vegetables, bok choy (or *pak choi*) has been cultivated in China since the fifth century A.D. and in the West since the mid-eighteenth century. Despite its ancient lineage, there still is some confusion about what exactly bok choy is. The name *bok choy* simply means "white vegetable" in Cantonese. This may be one reason why I often find my students confused as to whether bok choy and napa cabbage (*siu choy*) are the same vegetable. Both vegetables are Chinese cabbages, but they are different species and there *is* a difference in taste. To make matters more confusing, when this vegetable first became available in American supermarkets, I remember seeing bunches of bok choy— white stems only—in the produce section. All the beautiful green leaves had been chopped off! Today in supermarkets large and small bunches of bok choy come complete with white stems and green leaves, just as they do in Asian markets.

Bok choy comes in loose heads of eight to ten leaves measuring in height from 4 to 20 inches; Baby bok choy bunches are a little tighter, usually 3 to 4 inches thick.

There are four basic kinds of bok choy, differing in shape and size but easily identified as bok choy by the very white color of the stem and the broad green leaves. All varieties are also known as baby bok choy when harvested small.

Baby Bok Choy (see page 2 for Bok Choy)

Long-stemmed bok choy with flat green leaves, usually in large heads about 12 inches long

2 Bok choy with white spoon-shaped stems and slightly cupped shorter leaves, about 8 inches long

3 The smallest bok choy, usually 4 to 6 inches tall, known as squat or Canton type; this variety is often harvested as baby bok choy

4 The distinctive green-stemmed bok choy called Shanghai bok choy, which is usually available in the cold months

Dried bok choy is also used as an ingredient in cooking. In villages all over China, bunches of long-stemmed bok choy hanging to dry on a clothesline are a quaint and picturesque sight. If you grow your own bok choy, you might like to try this. Dried bok choy (*choy gonn*) is wonderful in soups.

How to Use

When cooking any variety of fresh bok choy, I like to separate the stems from the leaves, because the stems need to cook a little longer. The stems are juicy and taste delicately of cabbage—sweet but slightly sharp. The flavor of the leaves is more subtle. Bok choy leaves retain much of their vivid green color when cooked correctly and served promptly. I like to use them to wrap foods for steaming and to line steamer baskets when cooking dumplings. Baby bok choy, either white- or green-stemmed, are often cooked whole or halved lengthwise. Placed around the edges of a plate of steamed fish, they also make an attractive and tasty garnish.

When shopping for bok choy, you will often see that it has begun to flower. The flowering middle stems are edible and should be cooked with the stems. Bok choy can be eaten in all its stages of growth.

Because of its subtle flavor, bok choy can be used in stir-fries with beef, lamb, pork, poultry, and shellfish, or by itself, as well as in soups, braises, and steamed dishes. When young and tender, it is also good raw in salads.

Storage and Care

Buy fresh, crisp bok choy. It is best when used immediately, but to store, wrap bok choy loosely in a brown paper bag or paper towels, without washing, and store for one or two days in the vegetable bin of the refrigerator. To use, remove leaves and wash thoroughly in more than one change of water, because the tight stems tend to hold a fair amount of sandy grit. Drain and cut according to use.

Shanghai Bok Choy

Cultivation Tips

Although strictly speaking bok choy is biennial, it easily goes to seed under adverse conditions, so it is best to treat it as an annual. Bok choy is easy to grow and matures in five to eight weeks. The heads can be harvested at any stage of growth. Because it stands up to cold weather, it is best grown in late summer, fall, and even early winter. Like any shallow-rooted leafy greens with a high water content, bok choy requires moist, fertile soil and regular watering. Hot weather tends to make the plants bolt and toughen.

Scallop Mousse–Bok Choy Packets with Tomato Coulis

Yields 6 servings

Because the Chinese prefer small and baby bok choy, which they commonly use in stir-fries and soups, these are the sizes you will find in Chinatown and Asian markets. However, bok choy with large leaves is commonly available in nearly all supermarkets. The leaves remain a beautiful bright green when cooked, so I came up with this recipe, which is not only delicious but also very pretty.

6 large or 12 smaller bok choy, leaves and stems

FOR THE MOUSSE
1 pound sea scallops
$1/2$ pound flounder fillet
1 scallion, green and white parts cut into 2-inch pieces
2 teaspoons minced fresh ginger
1 teaspoon thin soy sauce
$1/2$ teaspoon salt
$1/2$ teaspoon freshly ground black pepper
4 large egg whites

•

6 medium whole shrimp, peeled and deveined
Salt and pepper
2 tablespoons Lemongrass Butter (page 168) or unsalted butter
Roasted Tomato Coulis (recipe follows)

Bring a large pot of water to a boil. Wash the bok choy leaves and cut the leaves from the stems. Cut the stems into sticks measuring 2 inches long by $1/4$ inch thick and set aside. Briefly blanch the leaves until limp but still bright green. Drain and refresh in ice water. Drain on paper towels and set aside.

Make the mousse. In a food processor, combine the scallops, fish, scallion, ginger, soy sauce, salt and pepper. Pulse until a smooth

See photograph on pages 10–11.

consistency. Add the egg whites and pulse until well combined. Place the mousse in a bowl and divide into 6 equal portions.

Lay out the bok choy leaves on a work surface. Spoon a portion of mousse onto each leaf, press a shrimp into the center of the mousse, and fold envelope-style to form a packet measuring about 3 x 4 inches. Repeat to form 6 packets.

Place half the bok choy stems on a 9-inch plate, sprinkle with additional salt and pepper to taste, and dot with ½ tablespoon of lemongrass butter. Lay 3 packets on top of the stems and dot with ½ tablespoon of butter. Place plate in one tier of the bamboo steamer. Repeat with remaining stems, butter, and packets on another plate.

Place the steamer tiers in a wok one-third full of water. Cover, bring to a boil, and steam 10 to 12 minutes, until fish packets feel firm to the touch and are just cooked through. Serve on individual plates accompanied by tomato coulis.

Roasted Tomato Coulis

Yields 1 cup

> 1½–2 pounds ripe plum tomatoes, washed
> Salt and freshly ground black pepper.

Preheat the oven to 400°F. Line a roasting pan with foil and place the tomatoes in the pan. Roast for 1 hour or until the tomatoes are wrinkled and very soft.

Remove the tomatoes to a strainer or food mill placed over a bowl. Scrape all the juice that has run out during cooking into the bowl. Push the tomatoes through the strainer or food mill and discard the skin and seeds. Lightly salt and pepper to taste and serve with the fish packets.

Chinese Cabbage
Siu Choy, Wong Nga Bak · Shao Cai, Huang Ya Bai
Brassica rapa, Pekinensis group

Chinese cabbage inspired me to write this book. The many Chinese names for this cabbage—*sui choy, wong nga bak, wong bok, pe-tsai*—make for a lot of confusion to anyone looking for it. The English names are also confusing: Chinese, Celery, Peking, Tientsin, and napa cabbage. It is sometimes even referred to as bok choy. To add to the confusion, there are three varieties commonly available that look different, but in every other respect are the same vegetable. They are the tight barrel type, commonly called napa cabbage; a loose-headed napa type that looks much like a light green-leaved head of romaine lettuce; and the tall cylindrical type known as Peking cabbage. In fact, they are all Chinese cabbage.

Although there are references to Chinese cabbage in books as early as the fifth century B.C., the vegetable we know today is probably a cross between a bok choy and a turnip, because there is no evidence of a wild Chinese cabbage. A long growing season and easy cultivation, not to mention a mild sweet flavor, has probably made this the most popular and readily available vegetable throughout China. It was introduced to Japan in the 1860s and was probably brought to North America by immigrant laborers late in the 1800s. Chinese cabbage is used to make the famous Korean pickle, *kim chee*.

I never had eaten Chinese cabbage raw until I came to live in the United States. Once I tried it, however, I became an ardent fan of the shredded cabbage in salads. The leaves keep their crisp texture for a long time and they have a sweet flavor that improves any salad. I like to use shredded dressed cabbage as a bed for a main-dish salad of chicken, smoked fish, or seafood.

Although there are three forms of Chinese cabbage, it is commonly available in only two. The tight-headed, barrel-shaped type (*siu choy*) is pale yellow-green and grows in heads 10 to 12 inches long and 5 to 6 inches around. The long cylindrical variety (*wong nga bak*) has broad leaf stalks and slightly crinkly leaves that are light to jade green. The 12- to 18-inch-long heads are looser than the barrel type, and usually measure 3 to 4 inches across. Both types have a very mild cabbage flavor, tastier than lettuce.

Chinese Cabbage, barrel type

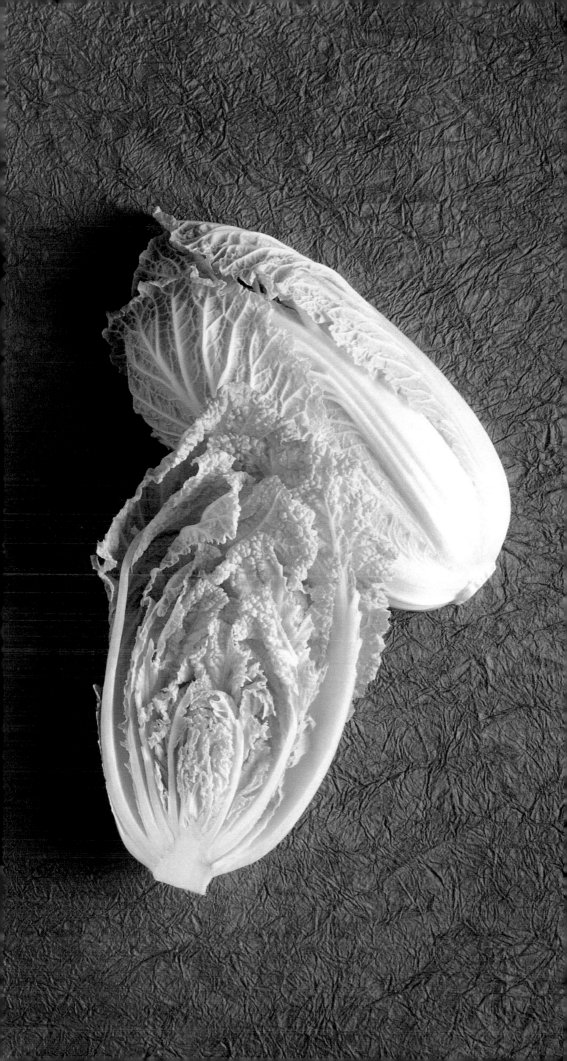

How to Use

Chinese cabbage is crisp and crunchy when served raw in salads. It retains its sweet flavor when braised, steamed, baked, boiled, or stir-fried. Long, slow cooking enhances its flavor. There is a famous Northern Chinese winter dish in which mounded leaves are slowly braised in broth until they are meltingly sweet, resulting in a dish not unlike the French onion confit. When blanched, the large leaves make excellent wrappers for various fillings, particularly fish or seafood.

Storage and Care

When buying Chinese cabbage, squeeze the heads to find a firm, heavy one. It keeps very well and can be stored in the vegetable bin for several weeks. The Chinese think that even when slightly wilted, the flavor improves and sweetens. Before using, cut off 1 to 2 inches at the base and rinse well in cold water. Do not be concerned if there are tiny black spots on the leaves. They occur naturally, and are harmless.

Cultivation Tips

Chinese cabbage should be grown in rich, fertile soil with regular watering. It has a tendency to bolt if sown too early and is exposed to frost or low temperatures, although there are varieties suited to early spring sowing. Most Chinese cabbages thrive when sown in late spring and early summer for a fall crop of full, firm heads.

Meatballs Braised in Chinese Cabbage

Yields 4 servings

This recipe is a variation on the traditional giant Chinese meatballs called lions' heads. I like this smaller size because they are easier to serve. It is best to make this dish in a covered casserole that can be brought to the table, so the cabbage "lid" is not disturbed before serving.

1 head Chinese cabbage (*siu choy* or *wong nga bak*), about 2 pounds

FOR THE MEATBALLS
4 dried Chinese black mushrooms
2 tablespoons dried tree ears (*wan yee*)
1 pound ground pork
1/2 cup diced jicama or fresh water chestnuts
1 teaspoon minced fresh ginger
2 scallions, green and white parts, minced
1 teaspoon minced orange zest
1 tablespoon dark soy sauce
1 tablespoon sherry
2 teaspoons cornstarch

1 teaspoon salt
1 teaspoon sugar
1 teaspoon freshly ground black pepper
1 large egg

FOR THE SAUCE
¼ cup dark soy sauce
2 tablespoons sherry
1½ cups unsalted or low-sodium chicken stock or water
1 teaspoon Szechuan peppercorns
1 2-inch piece orange peel
2 tablespoons vegetable oil
2 teaspoons cornstarch, mixed with 1 tablespoon cold water

Rinse the cabbage, cut off the base, and remove 16 whole leaves.
Shred the remaining cabbage and reserve.

Make the meatballs. In 2 small bowls, soak the mushrooms and
tree ears in warm water until soft, about 15 minutes. Drain the
mushrooms, reserving the soaking liquid. Cut off the stems and
discard, and coarsely chop the mushrooms. Drain the tree ears and
coarsely chop.

In a large bowl, combine the mushrooms, tree ears, pork, jicama,
ginger, scallions, orange zest, soy sauce, sherry, cornstarch, salt, sugar,
pepper, and egg. Mix well to combine. Form into 16 to 18 meatballs,
about the size of golf balls.

Make the sauce. In a small bowl, combine the reserved mushroom
liquid with the soy sauce, sherry, stock, Szechuan peppercorns, and
orange peel and set aside.

Using 8 cabbage leaves, line a heavy cast-iron casserole with 2
layers of leaves.

Heat the oil in a large skillet and brown the meatballs, a few at a
time, transferring them to the casserole as they are done. Pour the
sauce over the meatballs, cover with the shredded cabbage, then use
the remaining 8 leaves to cover in a double layer. Place the lid on the
casserole, bring the liquid to a boil, reduce heat to low, and simmer 40
to 45 minutes, until the cabbage is meltingly tender and the meatballs
are thoroughly cooked, firm to the touch. Add the cornstarch mixture
to the sauce. Return to a boil and simmer until the sauce thickens.

Bring the casserole to the table and serve the meatballs and
cabbage over steamed white rice.

Flowering Cabbage
Choy Sum · Cai Xin
Brassica parachinensis

When I was a girl, we lived on mainland Hong Kong, known as Kow-
loontong. We used to be taken on day-long expeditions to Hong Kong
island for clothes or to see the doctor several times a year. We looked
forward to these excursions, because we knew that at the end of the
day, we would be taken for a special treat, which we hoped would be
"chow mein." (Chinese Chow Mein is a dish of pan-fried noodles, not
the crispy noodles that go by that name in North America.)

Sometimes we would go to the Dairy Farm, Hong Kong's
equivalent to a soda fountain, for ice cream while the grown-ups had
English-style tea. If we were very hungry, however, we would beg for
chow mein. We would head for a favorite tea parlor, where we would
be served cups of piping hot, refreshing green tea while we waited for
our favorite pan-fried noodles topped with stir-fried beef and flowering
cabbage. The memory of those tasty noodles with soft tender beef and
crisp stems still makes my mouth water. The pretty, yellow-flowered
stems justify this vegetable's romantic name of "vegetable heart,"
because the "hearts" are the tastiest part.

Flowering cabbage is recognized by its slightly grooved, tender
green stems with characteristic small yellow flowers. The tender stems
are 6 to 8 inches long and $1/4$ to $1/2$ inch thick. The bright green oval
leaves vary in size, but generally are about 2 to 3 inches across and 4
to 5 inches long. The flowering stems are the best part, but the leaves
are used as well. Flowering cabbage has a delicate, sweet, slightly cab-
bagelike flavor and requires minimal cooking to maintain its crunch.

How to Use
Flowering cabbage is available year-round. It is the perfect all-purpose
vegetable for stir-fried dishes, whether you are using it with beef, pork,
chicken, or shrimp, as it requires only a few minutes of cooking. It is
often used in noodle dishes and makes a delicious vegetable stir-fry
when flavored with oyster sauce. It can be boiled or steamed and seasoned with a few drops of roasted sesame oil or other flavored oil. The
very young flowering stems may also be used raw in salad.

Storage and Care
Buy tender, young flowering cabbage that you can pierce easily. Store it
loosely wrapped in paper towels, then bagged in plastic, in the vegetable

bin of the refrigerator. Use within a day or two. To clean, soak in plenty of cold water, loosening the outer leaves at the stem to remove grit. If small leave whole to cook, or chop as desired. Do not peel stems.

Cultivation Tips

Flowering cabbage, like bok choy, requires moist, fertile soil and plenty of regular watering. There is a variety of purple-flowering *choy sum*, sometimes referred to as purple *pak choy* (in Cantonese, called *hong* (red) *choy sum* or *hong tsai tay*), which I have not seen in vegetable markets here, but seeds are available for the home gardener. This type has purple flowers and leaf stalks and leaves that can be purple or green. It is a cold-weather plant, and besides being very tasty, makes a beautiful ornamental plant during the cooler months.

Sesame-Flavored Flowering Cabbage

Yields 4 servings

This recipe works well with the baby flowering cabbage commonly available in the spring as well as with more mature plants. It is quick, easy, and delicious, and the pretty blossoms provide their own garnish. This is also delicious flavored with oyster sauce.

> 1 pound flowering cabbage (*choy sum*)
> 1 tablespoon vegetable oil
> 1 slice fresh ginger
> 2 tablespoons water
> 1 tablespoon thin soy sauce
> Pinch of sugar
> 1 tablespoon black or white sesame seeds, toasted
> 2 teaspoons roasted sesame oil

Wash the flowering cabbage thoroughly in cold water. Drain. Separate stems from leaves and flowering hearts.

Heat the oil in a wok, add the ginger, and brown to flavor the oil slightly. Remove and discard the ginger. Add the stems and stir-fry 30 seconds, tossing frequently. Add the leaves and hearts, and continue tossing to coat well, then quickly add the water. Cover the wok and turn the heat down slightly so the vegetables do not burn. Steam about 3 to 5 minutes, until the stems are tender.

Remove the cover from the wok. Add the soy sauce and sugar. Toss to blend and flavor, then sprinkle with the sesame seeds. Turn off the heat, drizzle on the sesame oil, turn once or twice, and serve.

Flat Cabbage
Tatsoi (Japanese), Tai Goo Choy (Chinese) · Tai Gu Cai
Brassica rosularis

太古菜

This flat, plate-shaped cabbage is another cousin of bok choy. It grows only a few inches from the ground to a diameter of 5 to 14 inches. Like bok choy, the stems are white, but the leaves are thicker and darker, almost black in color. At present, the mature vegetable is rarely available in markets, but several catalogs list seeds for the home gardener. Recently, while shopping at one of New York's great specialty markets, Balducci's, I saw a whole case of baby *tai goo choy* leaves, all washed and ready for the salad bowl. While the leaves were very young and the flavor delicate, they had a sweet juiciness that would enhance any salad. Flat cabbage is more commonly sold as one of several baby greens in a salad mix and more readily available wholesale than at the retail level. The Chinese prefer flat cabbage in its mature form and like it cooked.

The most common Asian name for flat cabbage is the Japanese, *tatsoi*. Be careful not to confuse this vegetable with *choy sum* (flowering cabbage), because the names are similar in colloquial Cantonese.

How to Use
Flat cabbage tastes like bok choy; in its mature form it has a stronger flavor than bok choy. It is excellent raw in salads when picked very young. Because of flat cabbage's sharper flavor, it can be used in many dishes where arugula is called for, but it is sweeter than arugula and does not have its bite. Flat cabbage is very good simply stir-fried with ginger and soy, but it can be sautéed in olive oil or butter, steamed, boiled, and used in soups.

Storage and Care
Like boy choy, flat cabbage should be used within a day or two, or stored loosely wrapped in paper in the vegetable bin of the refrigerator. The leaves should be separated and washed carefully in several changes of water, because this squat vegetable tends to be very gritty. Use flat cabbage in any dish that calls for bok choy.

Cultivation Tips
Flat cabbage is extremely tolerant of cold and seed can be sown in early spring and late summer—even in autumn for a winter crop. It matures in four to five weeks, but the baby cabbage can be picked for

salads after a couple of weeks. These shallow-rooted plants need fertile soil and regular watering, as does bok choy.

Wilted Flat Cabbage Salad

Yields 4 servings

A few years ago, flat cabbage was seldom seen in markets here, but it is now very popular in its baby stage, particularly in salads. The hot dressing makes the cabbage wilt slightly, but it remains succulent and crunchy. The amounts given for the dressing are generous—the salad is delicious when drenched with it—but you may choose to use it sparingly. Any leftover dressing will make a wonderful dip for dumplings, and will keep for a week or longer in the refrigerator.

> 1 pound baby flat cabbage (*tatsoi* or *tai goo choy*)
>
> FOR THE DRESSING:
> ¼ cup hot chili oil
> 2 teaspoons minced fresh ginger
> 2 garlic cloves, minced
> 4 tablespoons minced scallions, green and white parts
> ½ cup rice vinegar
> ¼ cup roasted sesame oil
> ⅓ cup thin soy sauce
> ½ cup Ginger Broth (page 98)
> 2 tablespoons brown sugar

Wash the cabbage leaves well and dry in a salad spinner. Place in a heavy ceramic or wooden salad bowl.

Make the dressing. Heat the chili oil in a small saucepan. Add the ginger, garlic, and scallions and toss 10 seconds or until aromatic. Add the vinegar, sesame oil, soy sauce, ginger broth, and brown sugar Bring to a simmer and stir gently until sugar is dissolved.

Pour hot dressing over cabbage salad, toss to blend, and serve.

Oil Seed Rape
Yau Choy · You Cai
Brassica rapa, Chinesis group

When I find myself in Chinatown at lunchtime, I often stop at my
favorite Chinese cafe for a quick one-dish meal. In Chinatowns
everywhere you will see cafes with rows of roasted and poached
ducks, chickens, spare-ribs, marinated pork, and even part of a crispy-
skinned whole roast pig hanging in the windows. This is the Chinese
equivalent of deli food, and a simple, inexpensive dish of rice topped
with pieces of roast duck or pork is Chinese fast food at its best. A side
order of *yau choy* (literally oil vegetable) is the perfect way to balance
your meal.

The Chinese like to present these greens blanched, cut into 3- or
4-inch lengths, and piled, perfectly aligned, on a plate, then drizzled
with oyster sauce and roasted sesame oil. The glistening bright green
stalks contrasting with the dark sauce are a perfect illustration of the
principles of yin and yang in food presentation. As you pick up the
first crunchy green stalk, you know that eating this oil seed rape can
only be good for you.

Rape is best known for its seed, which is used to make rape seed
(canola) oil. I like to use this Chinese flowering vegetable sautéed with
garlic and olive oil in a pasta dish. Oil seed rape is much sweeter than
broccoli rabe and I find them a perfect fit for pasta.

How to Use
Be sure to wash well. Both leaves and stalks are edible and the
flowering center stalks are particularly succulent. Rape greens are best
when the vegetable is quickly blanched in boiling water, cooled, and
steamed, or they can be blanched and stir-fried or sautéed without
blanching. They should be cooked quickly and served when just
tender but still crunchy.

Storage and Care
Store in an open plastic or paper bag or loosely wrapped in paper
towels in vegetable bin of the refrigerator. Wash just prior to use. Rape
greens will keep several days or up to one week if very fresh.

Cultivation Tips
Rape seeds should be sown shallow where they are to grow; do not
transplant. The fast-growing seedlings can be thinned as the plants

grow to about 18 inches. The leaves have a slightly oiled or glazed look to them. They like well-drained, fertile soil and do well in temperate climates. They are shallow-rooted and should be watered frequently. Plants mature in 40 to 60 days.

Rape Greens with Oyster Sauce

Yields 4 servings

In Chinatown restaurants you will find rape greens served with the leaves mounded and the stems laid over them in a perfectly symmetrical pile. Oyster sauce is then drizzled over for a yin-yang effect of bright green and rich brown. If you like this look, you can arrange the rape greens on your serving dish, cover with waxed paper, cook it briefly in the microwave, then drizzle with the sauce and rewarm slightly—a perfect vegetable dish in minutes. In my recipe, this green is cooked in a wok, which is the traditional home-style way.

> 1 pound rape greens (*yau choy*)
> 2 teaspoons vegetable oil
> 1 slice fresh ginger
> ¼ cup unsalted or low-sodium chicken stock or water
> ½ teaspoon salt
> Pinch of sugar
> 2 tablespoons oyster sauce
> 2 teaspoons roasted sesame oil

Wash the greens thoroughly in cold water, trim, and cut the leaves from the stalks.

In a wok, heat the oil, add the ginger slice, and cook until the ginger is brown. Remove and discard the ginger. Add the stalks, stir-fry 1 minute, tossing frequently, then add the leaves and continue to stir-fry about 30 seconds. Add the stock, salt, and sugar, cover, and cook 2 to 3 minutes. Uncover and stir to blend. Test to see if stalks are tender with the point of a knife. If not, cook, covered, another minute or two, until stalks are tender but still crisp.

Uncover the wok, add the oyster sauce, and stir to blend well. Turn off heat, drizzle with sesame oil, and serve.

Chinese Broccoli
Gai Lan · Jie Lan
Brassica oleracea, Alboglabra group

芥蘭

When my daughter, Sam, was small, her favorite Chinese dish was beef and broccoli. I always wondered if Sam loved the taste of broccoli or just the pretty white flowers on Chinese broccoli stems. In any case, I never asked her, because her love of this dish made her eat all her broccoli, even when I used regular broccoli in the dish. (Getting Sam to eat her vegetables was not a problem!) Serving Chinese broccoli may be the answer to your child's "Ugh! I hate broccoli."

Chinese broccoli was introduced to China in ancient times, quite possibly by the Portuguese (it is a close relative of Portuguese cabbage). *Gai lan* has smooth stems, about ¼ to ¾ inch thick, with blue-green leaves and small white buds and flowers. It is usually 8 to 10 inches long. As its name suggests, it has a delicate broccoli taste and is sweet and succulent. Every part of the vegetable—leaves, stems, buds, and flowers—is delectable.

How to Use
Chinese broccoli can be steamed, boiled, stir-fried, and used in all dishes calling for broccoli. It should be washed briefly to remove any grit, and any tough stems can be peeled. I often separate the leaves from the stalks, and if using in a stir-fry, will blanch the stems first. A dash of wine or spirits and a pinch of sugar will enhance its flavor and bring out the natural sweetness.

Storage and Care
When shopping for Chinese broccoli, look for unblemished leaves and more buds than opened flowers on the central stalk. Store in the vegetable bin of the refrigerator, lightly wrapped in paper, for up to a week. Do not wash until just ready to use.

Cultivation Tips
This fast-growing annual is very easy to grow. Although it likes the cooler weather of spring and fall—ideal times for sowing—it will tolerate warmer and colder weather and matures in just under three months. When the plant is 8 to 10 inches tall with stalks measuring about ¾ inch thick, it can be cut. It is best cut before too many buds open. The plant will resprout after one harvest. If left to flower, Chinese broccoli makes a beautiful ornamental plant.

Yields 2 to 4 servings

Although beef with broccoli appears on most North American Chinese restaurant menus, very few customers have tasted the authentic dish. You must use Chinese broccoli (*gai lan*). Chinese broccoli has tiny white flowers on the central stalk, so the dish does not even look like the run-of-the-mill take-out beef with broccoli!

1½ pounds Chinese broccoli (*gai lan*)

FOR THE MARINADE:
1 tablespoon dark soy sauce
1 tablespoon cornstarch
2 teaspoons dry white wine

•

1 pound flank steak
3 tablespoons vegetable oil
1 garlic clove, minced
1 teaspoon minced fresh ginger
1 scallion, green and white parts minced
1 tablespoon dark soy sauce
¼ cup unsalted or low-sodium chicken stock or water
1 tablespoon brandy
½ teaspoon sugar
2 teaspoons roasted sesame oil

Wash the broccoli well in cold water, separating the leaves and tender hearts and the stalks. Peel the thicker stalks, if necessary. Set aside.

Make the marinade. Mix the soy sauce, cornstarch, and wine in a bowl. Slice the beef across the grain into ¼-inch-thick pieces about 1½ inches long. Combine with the marinade and let stand at least 10 minutes.

Heat 1 tablespoon oil in a wok and stir-fry the broccoli stalks, about 30 seconds to 1 minute, then add the leaves and hearts and stir-fry another 30 seconds, tossing frequently. Remove to a bowl and set aside.

Return wok to the heat and add the remaining 2 tablespoons oil. Over medium-high heat, stir-fry the garlic, ginger, and scallion for 30 seconds, or until aromatic. Add the beef and stir-fry until browned, tossing frequently. Add the soy sauce, stock, brandy, and sugar, then the broccoli, tossing to blend and heating the broccoli. Turn off heat, drizzle with sesame oil, and serve.

Mizuna
Siu cai · Xiu Cai
Brassica rapa, Japonica group

Whenever my friend Brad Ogden—a well-known California chef—is in New York, I make it a point of working with him. Brad made his reputation cooking great American food, and he can usually be counted on to be using the freshest, the best, and the "newest" American ingredients. Once, while helping Brad prepare for a demonstration class, I was surprised and delighted to be asked to clean a box of mizuna. The main course that day was a wonderful pork loin braised in a roasted tomato broth. Brad lightly and quickly wilted the mizuna, which, with its earthy fresh taste, was a perfect complement to the rich pork.

Mizuna is easily recognized by the feathery, jagged edges of its green leaves. Although it grows in a bushy clump and can be left to mature into a deep green head, measuring up to 9 inches high and 18 inches across, it is most often sold in separate leaves that have been harvested while tender and young. The young leaves measure as little as 1½ inches long and about 1 inch across. You will often find it in a mix of baby greens, or mesclun. Young mizuna is reminiscent of arugula, but the taste is much milder and sweeter. The stalks, particularly in more mature forms, are quite juicy.

How to Use
Tender little mizuna leaves are excellent raw in salads, which is how it is usually used here. However, mizuna is also very good steamed, stir-fried, or quickly wilted with a bit of garlic and a dash of oil. Mature mizuna is also a good substitute for kale or chard; it can be used in various kinds of stuffings.

Storage and Care
A delicate leafy green, mizuna should be stored in the vegetable bin of the refrigerator. It will wilt easily and should be used within a day or two of purchase, particularly if intended for salads. Rinse briefly in cold water if required.

Cultivation Tips
Mizuna is both heat and frost resistant and grows well in any fertile soil with a reasonable amount of moisture. It can be sown from spring to late fall, with several plantings. Leaves will be ready for cutting in two to three weeks.

Although I have not encountered it in Chinatown markets, several seed catalogs list a close relative of mizuna, known as mibuna. It differs from mizuna in that its long, narrow, smooth-edged leaves grow into a spray up to 22 inches across and 12 to 18 inches high at maturity. Its taste is a little sharper than mizuna, but the vegetable can be cultivated and used in the same way.

Wilted Mizuna with Balsamic Vinegar

Yields 4 servings

Mizuna is commonly served in salads and has a slight peppery flavor. I like to wilt it quickly and serve it with lamb chops or a rich pork roast.

> 2 tablespoons extra-virgin olive oil
> 2 garlic cloves, mashed
> 1 pound mizuna (*sui cai*)
> 1 teaspoon salt
> ½ teaspoon black pepper
> ¼ teaspoon sugar
> 1 tablespoon balsamic vinegar

Heat the oil in a skillet, add the garlic, and toss a few seconds. Add the mizuna, stir, and sprinkle with salt, pepper, and sugar. Toss constantly until the mizuna is wilted. Drizzle with balsamic vinegar, stir to blend, and serve.

Wrapped Heart Mustard Cabbage
Dai Gai Choy · Da Jie Cai
Brassica juncea var. *rugosa*

芥
菜

When I was a girl, pickled wrapped heart mustard cabbage was my favorite vegetable. Whenever I knew that the main dish would be something I would not eat (such as my sister's favorite dish, steamed pork cake), I would sneak into the kitchen and beg the cook to make up a dish with pickled wrapped heart mustard cabbage. The cook would make a quick stir-fried dish by throwing together bits of trimmings from the pork and chopped pickled mustard cabbage, seasoned with soy sauce and a bit of sugar. The pungent flavor, with its crunchy sharpness, was a perfect balance for the bland, steaming hot rice that was served at every meal. I still think pickled mustard cabbage makes a perfect, simple fast lunch, and sometimes I top it off with a bowl of soup made of fresh mustard cabbage in hot broth.

Wrapped heart mustard cabbage is easy to identify: it looks like a large loose-headed green cabbage. It is sometimes called headed mustard cabbage or large-leafed mustard greens, or Swatow heart mustard cabbage. The leafy greens are sometimes trimmed off, leaving only the rounded stalks. It is a darker green than a regular green cabbage, but not as green as a savoy cabbage. Clean, firm, heavy heads are best. Pungency and sharpness vary, but as its name suggests, this vegetable has a sharp, mustardy taste.

How to Use
Fresh wrapped heart mustard cabbage is best used in soups. Wash well, remove any coarse and damaged leaves, halve, and chop as for slaw or cut into chunks. It should be cooked until softened, so it is best used in long-cooking soups you make from scratch. Stir-fry bits of pork and bones, or other meat, add water, and bring to a rolling boil before adding cut-up mustard cabbage. Simmer one hour or longer. This is also an ideal green to use in duck soup, using a chopped roast duck or a duck carcass from Peking duck.

Storage and Care
As with green cabbage, it is best to store the mustard cabbage loosely wrapped in paper in the vegetable bin of the refrigerator. In a pinch, they will keep a few days in a cool room. If they lose crispness, do not be overly concerned. Do not wash until ready to use.

Cultivation Tips

Because mustard cabbages are large, full plants, they require room to grow and are best sown outdoors. Shallow-sow in fertile, moisture-retentive soil. Seedlings should be spaced 10 to 12 inches apart and you should allow three to four months for them to mature. They grow best in warm weather, but will tolerate cold well. In temperate climates, sow the seed in spring or early summer for a fall or winter crop. In warmer climates, the seeds can be sown in the fall for a late winter or spring crop. The greens should be harvested when mature for full development of flavor. I don't recommend picking for salads if small.

Hot and Sour Wrapped Heart Mustard Cabbage Soup

Yields 4 to 6 servings

This mustard cabbage is most often used for making pickles, but it is also good when cooked for a long time in soup. The cabbage seems to sweeten with wilting and slow cooking, and its flavor mellows, so this is one vegetable you don't need to keep crisp. I have made this soup hot and sour because these flavors are so popular, and the hearty soup that results is great on a cold day.

1½ pounds swatow mustard cabbage (*dai gai choy*)
2 teaspoons vegetable oil
1 teaspoon minced fresh ginger
4 cups unsalted or low-sodium meat, chicken, or vegetable stock (water will do)
¼ cup cider vinegar
1 teaspoon thin soy sauce
¼ teaspoon cayenne pepper, or to taste
2 squares (½ pound) tofu, preferably soft
Salt and freshly ground black pepper
2 teaspoons cornstarch, mixed with 2 tablespoons cold water
1 large egg, beaten

Wash the mustard cabbage and separate leaves to clean thoroughly. Cut coarsely and set aside.

In a deep saucepan or pot, heat the oil and stir-fry the ginger until aromatic, about 30 seconds. Add the mustard cabbage and the stock, bring to a boil, and simmer over low heat for 40 minutes.

Add the vinegar, soy sauce, and cayenne, and simmer another 20 minutes.

Cut the tofu into cubes and add to the soup. Simmer another 10 minutes. Add salt and pepper to taste. Pour the cornstarch mixture into the soup and stir until it thickens. Turn off the heat and stir in the beaten egg with a fork just before serving.

Bamboo Mustard Cabbage
Juk Gai Choy · Zhu Jie Cai
Brassica juncea var. *foliosa*

Last winter, on an icy cold day, I was delighted to see bunches of this distinctive mustard cabbage in a Chinatown market. Farther down the block, I bought two squares of soft tofu.

Rushing home, I put a pot of water on to boil while I washed the greens, then I blanched them so they would taste sweet and be tender. I laid the vegetable on a plate, cut the squares of tofu into cubes, and placed them over the bed of greens. Oyster sauce, a bit of pepper, and a drizzle of roasted sesame oil, and the dish was ready to be steamed. In ten minutes, I sat down to a tasty hot lunch. I am no vegetarian, but this dish satisfied me completely.

Bamboo mustard cabbage is easy to recognize. The bunches look like very small loose-leaved heads of romaine, but the green leaves have serrated edges. The single taproot is usually attached. The heads are from 6 to 12 inches long. In Hong Kong *juk gai choy* is considered sweeter than other mustard cabbages (when properly handled, of course), but the vegetable retains a characteristic mustard flavor.

How to Use
Bamboo mustard cabbage should be washed well, leaves separated, and cut, if large, to desired lengths. The leaves can be steamed and stir-fried, but only after parboiling or blanching. It is very good in soups.

Storage and Care
Store in the vegetable bin of the refrigerator for up to one week, wrapped in paper towels or a brown paper bag. Do not wash until ready to use.

Cultivation Tips
Cultivate as for Swatow mustard cabbage. It's best to sow the seed in summer and autumn, which allows the stems to develop in cool weather. The greens can be harvested in about 40 days.

Chicken Rolls Filled with Bamboo Mustard Cabbage

Yields 4 servings

4 thin chicken cutlets, about 1½ pounds
1½ teaspoons salt
½ teaspoon freshly ground black pepper
1 cup Bamboo Mustard Cabbage Filling (recipe follows)

1 tablespoon olive oil
4 tablespoons white wine
Roasted Tomato Coulis (page 17)

Preheat the oven to 350°F.

Pound the chicken cutlets between 2 sheets of waxed paper until very thin. Be careful not to break the chicken and form holes.

Sprinkle both sides of each cutlet with salt and pepper. Spread each cutlet with ¼ cup of filling, but do not spread all the way to the edge. Roll up each cutlet as for a jelly roll and tie with kitchen string.

Rub the chicken rolls with olive oil and set on a baking sheet. Sprinkle the rolls with 2 tablespoons of the wine and bake 10 minutes. Turn each roll and sprinkle with the remaining 2 tablespoons wine. Continue cooking until the chicken is completely cooked through and firm to the touch, another 15 to 20 minutes. The chicken rolls will remain mostly white.

Remove string and serve rolls with tomato coulis.

Bamboo Mustard Cabbage Filling

Yields about 2⅓ cups

2 pounds bamboo mustard cabbage (*chuk gai choy*)
2 teaspoons olive oil
1 large onion (sweet if possible), minced (about 2½ cups)
1 tablespoon minced fresh ginger
½ cup white wine
½ cup unsalted or low-sodium chicken stock
1 teaspoon salt
¼ teaspoon black pepper
2 tablespoons heavy cream
2 tablespoons dry bread crumbs

Wash the mustard cabbage in plenty of cold water and separate the leaves from the stems. Discard the stems or save for another use. Cut leaves into thin ribbons. You should have about 7 cups. In a skillet, heat the olive oil and sauté the onion over medium heat, stirring often, until soft and tender, about 10 minutes. Add the ginger and cook a few seconds, then add the wine, stock, and salt and pepper. Add the cabbage and cook over medium heat for 10 to 15 minutes, until tender. Remove the vegetables with a slotted spoon and set aside. Over high heat, reduce the cooking liquid to about 2 tablespoons. In a food processor, pulse the vegetables until coarsely chopped. Add the reduced cooking liquid, cream, and bread crumbs. Pulse to blend well. Remove to a bowl and refrigerate until cold before using.

Amaranth
Een Choy · Xian Cai
Amaranthus tricolor

In the late spring and early summer, one can always find both kinds of
Chinese spinach or amaranth in Chinatown—the common green
variety and the beautiful red type. My professional cooking students
always want to buy red amaranth, even though most of them don't
know what it is. They always say, "It will make a great garnish!"

One class was fortunate to include Melody Santos, a student from
the Philippines, who was familiar with the vegetable. She volunteered
to prepare a dish with red amaranth. She rushed from stall to stall,
buying a green papaya, some hot chilies, garlic, onion, ginger, an
exotic black chicken, and the red amaranth. At lunchtime, Melody
presented to each of us a steaming bowl of soup with sweet lumps of
papaya and leaves of amaranth floating in a beautiful pink broth,
colored by the red leaves. Not only was it pretty, it tasted wonderful,
with a sweet, fresh, slightly hot flavor.

Amaranth grows on a slender stem with clusters of oval, soft,
slightly rough-textured leaves. The clusters are usually 5 to 8 inches
long, but can be smaller or larger. The leaves tend to go limp easily, so
the vegetable is usually sold with the roots intact. The leaves of the
green variety can be light or dark green, while the red variety has deep
red, almost burgundy colored, markings that spread from the center of
the leaves and fade into dark green around the edges.

Amaranth tastes a little like spinach, but has more texture and
body and a flavor of the earth. Both stems and leaves have a slightly
rough texture but are completely edible. Amaranth originated in South
America but has been cultivated as a food crop in Asia for centuries.
Because it is a warm-climate plant, it is at its best from early summer
on through the fall.

How to Use
Cut off the roots and wash the leaves thoroughly. Use both stems and
leaves; older stems can be trimmed and cut. If you grow amaranth, the
very young tender leaves are especially good in salads. This is a highly
nutritious green, rich in vitamins A and C, iron, calcium, and protein.
Although amaranth is frequently cooked like spinach, I think it tastes
best in soups. However, the Chinese prepare it by stir-frying, sautéing,
and steaming. Cook amaranth quickly, just until wilted.

Storage and Care

Amaranth, green or red, is best used within a day or two. For maximum life, it is best wrapped in damp paper towels and loosely bagged in the refrigerator vegetable bin. Just before using, trim off the roots and any coarse stems. Separate larger leaves and wash in several waters if very gritty. My favorite way of washing *een choy* (or any very gritty vegetable) is to fill a large basin with tepid water in which a few drops of oil are added; this helps the grit sink to the bottom. Wash and rinse until free of grit.

Cultivation Tips

Amaranth is a hot-weather annual and does best in climates with summer temperatures between 68 and 90°F. Sow the seeds in fertile, well-drained, slightly sandy soil in late spring or early to late summer. Plants can be picked very young to eat raw, or harvested at maturity in six to eight weeks.

Spicy Amaranth

Yields 2 to 4 servings

A very pretty vegetable, amaranth is commonly used in soups, where it turns the broth a rosy color. This recipe for stir-fried amaranth in fragrant spices is a nice change.

> 1 pound red amaranth (*een choy*)
> 1 teaspoon ground cumin
> 1/2 teaspoon ground coriander
> 1/2 teaspoon ground cloves
> 1/2 teaspoon ground cardamom
> 2 tablespoons vegetable oil
> 1 garlic clove, minced
> 1 teaspoon minced fresh ginger
> 1 small jalapeño pepper, seeded and minced
> 1 teaspoon salt
> 1 tablespoon lime juice

Wash the amaranth thoroughly, removing and discarding any tough stalk ends. Spin-dry in a salad spinner and set aside.

Combine the cumin, coriander, cloves, and cardamom in a small bowl.

Heat the oil in a wok over medium-high heat. Add the garlic, ginger, and jalapeño and toss for 10 seconds. Add the cumin mixture and continue stirring a few seconds until aromatic, then add the amaranth, salt, lime juice, and 2 tablespoons of water. Stir-fry just until the vegetables wilt, 1 to 2 minutes. Remove from heat and serve.

Garland Chrysanthemum
Tun Ho · Tong Hao
Chrysanthemum coronarium

Walking through Chinatown on a freezing day, I saw piles of garland chrysanthemum, which brought back memories of my childhood. At least once every winter our cook would welcome us to a Cantonese hotpot dinner. Bubbling broth is presented at the table in a special pot with a chimney for the hot coals and a moat for the soup. Platters of thinly sliced meat, poultry, seafood, and cellophane noodles are placed around the pot along with mounds of garland chrysanthemum and other greens. Small dishes of different sauces—and sometimes a raw egg—are put in front of each diner, who picks up morsels of food, quickly cooks them in the broth, dips them into a sauce, and pops them into the mouth. As the meal progresses, the broth gets richer, but also cooks down. This is the time to add the chrysanthemum greens, because the liquid exuded by it replenishes the soup. At the end of the dinner, everyone enjoys a bowl of the delicious enriched soup.

Although other green leafy vegetables are used in a hotpot, I have always found the slightly perfumed taste of garland chrysanthemum greens perfect for the rich savory broth. The broad-leaf variety is favored by the Chinese. Other varieties are grown for both their edible leaves and their flowers.

Garland chrysanthemum is one of the most popular vegetables in Japan. The leaves are like those of ordinary garden chrysanthemum, except they are larger and a lighter green. In Asian markets, they are usually sold with the roots. The plants are not allowed to flower or grow too old, because the leaves become bitter. The vegetable bunches measure 2 to 4 inches across and are 5 to 8 inches long.

How to Use
Garland chrysanthemum can be used in soups, stir-fried with meats, or lightly boiled. The Japanese often blanch and refresh it before serving it cold as a salad, or batter-coat the leaves and make tempura. It should be cooked quickly because overcooking causes bitterness.

Storage and Care
Buy crisp greens with no buds or flowers. As with other leafy greens, store wrapped in paper or plastic for several days or up to one week in

Garland Chrysanthemum, broad-leaf type

the vegetable bin of the refrigerator. Separate the leaves and wash well just before using.

Cultivation Tips
This plant prefers cool weather and can even withstand light frosts. It likes a fertile, moist soil, but can take a little drought.

Seafood Broth with Garland Chrysanthemum

Yields 4 to 6 servings

The inspiration for this dish comes from a classic hotpot, cooked at the table and usually including seafood, meat, vegetables, and garland chrysanthemum. I decided to Westernize the recipe and ended up with a delicious low-fat main-dish soup, served with crusty country bread. For those of us who prefer a richer broth, you can dilute some cilantro pesto mayonnaise and add it just before serving the soup.

$1\frac{1}{2}$ pounds garland chrysanthemum (*tung ho*)
1 quart unsalted or low-sodium stock, preferably fish, but chicken will do
2 slices fresh ginger
1 scallion, green and white parts cut into 2-inch pieces
$1\frac{1}{2}$ tablespoons salt
$\frac{1}{2}$ teaspoon black pepper
2 tablespoons sherry
1 pound medium shrimp, peeled and deveined
12 ounces red snapper fillet, cut into 3-inch squares
2 medium squid (about 5 ounces total), cleaned and cut into rings
$\frac{1}{2}$ pound sea scallops
Cilantro Pesto Mayonnaise (optional; page 156)
Handful of cilantro sprigs, for garnish

Wash the chrysanthemum greens in plenty of cold water and trim off stems. Separate leaves. Set aside.

In a large pot or enameled casserole, heat the stock with the ginger and scallion. Cover and simmer for 10 minutes. With a slotted spoon, remove the ginger and scallion and discard. Season with salt, pepper, and sherry.

Add the greens and simmer for 5 minutes, or until tender.

Add the shrimp, cook gently for 1 minute, then add the red snapper and the squid. Continue to simmer until the fish just begins to turn white and opaque, about 3 minutes. Add the scallops and cook 30 seconds, or until they turn white.

Remove the pot from the heat. If you are adding the mayonnaise, thin with a little stock and stir into the soup, then immediately strew cilantro sprigs over the top and serve.

Water Spinach
Ong Choy · Weng Cai
Ipomoea aquatica

Several years ago, I visited my brother who now lives in Vancouver. Although we have a great Chinatown in New York, I had heard that the Chinese restaurants in Vancouver were the best outside China. On my first night, my brother promised me a great treat—dinner at his favorite restaurant with food just like in Hong Kong. The food was good, but I didn't find it superior to what I've found in New York's Chinatown until the water spinach appeared. He had asked for it to be prepared with salted shrimp paste, and it was certainly a treat; the hollow stems trap the sharp, salty shrimp flavor. Instantly, I was transported to my childhood. Before my trip to Vancouver, I had not found water spinach in New York, but a season or two later it was everywhere.

Water spinach, also called empty-hearted vegetable, is easily recognized by its hollow stems and flat arrow-shaped leaves, which measure anywhere from 1 to 8 inches long. There are two varieties, one a pale green and one a darker green, although the Chinese prefer the paler one for its sweeter flavor and so this is the variety most commonly found in Asian markets. Although water spinach is not botanically in the spinach family, it shares two common characteristics of spinach: a high water content and a tendency to shrink when cooked. The hollow stems trap flavor while the leaves wilt quickly. The flavor is delicate and fresh, and as with most of these green leafy vegetables, it is high in vitamins and minerals. The Chinese, however, value it for its texture and flavor rather than its tonic qualities.

How to Use

Wash briefly in cold water and cut off and discard 1 to 2 inches of the stems. Cut the stems into desired lengths and keep separate from leaves, so you can cook the stems a few minutes longer. Water spinach can be stir-fried alone, steamed, boiled, used in soups, and stir-fried with meat or seafood. My favorite method—and one that is popular with many Chinese—is to stir-fry the vegetable with garlic, ginger, salted shrimp paste or preserved tofu, and even a bit of spicy chili paste. This blending of the delicate sweet flavor of the water spinach with the sharp, strong taste of shrimp paste creates a balance that is much loved by the Chinese. Be sure to buy enough water spinach, because it loses a lot of bulk in cooking.

Storage and Use

Water spinach is very perishable and should be used within one to two days. It deteriorates rapidly, with the leaves turning yellow and mushy. Store in the vegetable bin of the refrigerator and wash just before using.

Cultivation Tips

Water spinach requires very warm temperatures and lots of water to grow. In China, it is often found on muddy banks. It is not feasible for the home garden, except possibly for one in the right climate and with suitably wet soil.

Three Ways with Water Spinach

Yields 4 servings

Because water spinach, much loved by nearly every one of my Chinese friends, has hollow stems that suck up flavor, it is most often stir-fried with shrimp paste or pickled tofu (*fu yee*). So this one basic recipe includes three variations using shrimp paste, spicy pickled tofu, or fish sauce. If you think these flavorings are too strong—and the shrimp paste certainly has a strong aroma—you might try substituting one or two anchovies mashed with the garlic.

> 1 pound water spinach (*ong choy*)
> 1 tablespoon vegetable oil
> 2 garlic cloves, minced
> 1 teaspoon minced fresh ginger
> 1 scallion, green and white parts minced
> 2 teaspoons shrimp paste, or 2 tablespoons pickled tofu with chili, or 2 tablespoons fish sauce (*nuoc mam* or *nam pla*)

Wash and trim the spinach in plenty of cold water. Separate the stems from the leaves and keep separate.

Heat the oil in a wok and add the garlic, ginger, and scallion. Stir-fry 30 seconds. Add the flavoring of choice, 1/4 cup water, and the spinach stems. Reduce the heat, cover, and simmer about 1 minute, or until stems are just tender. Add the leaves and stir-fry to wilt, tossing constantly. Cook 3 to 5 minutes, or until the spinach is soft and strongly flavored. Serve.

Slippery Vegetable
Saan Choy · Chan Cai
Basella alba

When it came to writing about slippery vegetable, my enthusiasm waned a bit. We always had this vegetable in soup, and although I loved the tofu and salt egg that usually went into the soup, I never liked the mucilaginous quality of the vegetable. When I thought about this, however, I was a little puzzled, because that is exactly what I like about okra. So I decided to try it blanched with a drizzle of olive oil and vinegar (which is how I serve okra) and I found it quite delicious.

Other names for slippery vegetable are Ceylon spinach or Malabar spinach. It originated in India, but has been popular with the Chinese for centuries. It is used throughout Southeast Asia because it grows easily in humid, tropical climates. There are several varieties of slippery vegetable, but the most common in Asian markets is *Basella alba*, with its bright green stems and leaves. The leaves are broadly oval, feel slightly rubbery, and are joined to the stem to form a very loose head. Slippery vegetable has an earthy, mild spinach flavor, and if you do not object to its "slippery" quality, it is tasty and highly nutritious.

How to Use

A summer vegetable, slippery vegetable is best used in soups, but it can be stir-fried, steamed, blanched, and used in stews and braises where its thickening properties are desired. Quick or short cooking times produce the best results; overlong cooking enhances its slimy qualities.

Storage and Care

Buy crisp heads with unblemished, bright green leaves. Store in the refrigerator vegetable bin for up to one week. Wash just before using and cut into desired lengths. If stir-frying, separate stalks from leaves as the stalks require a few minutes more cooking time.

Cultivation Tips

This is recommended for hot, humid climates where slippery vegetable will thrive as a perennial. It is also grown as an annual in temperate climates. Seed catalogs usually list it as Malabar spinach. Slippery vegetable needs high temperatures and long daylight hours and will not tolerate frost. Sow the seed in late spring or early summer in sandy loamy soil, rich in organic matter, then water well. The leaves are usually ready for harvesting in about 70 days.

Yields 4 servings

This bright green vegetable is aptly named in English, for it is distinctly slippery on the tongue. In this chicken soup it gives the broth an earthy taste. It is also good simply blanched, drained, flavored with salt and a good bit of freshly ground pepper, then drizzled with virgin olive oil and lemon juice. Because dirt tends to stick to the leaves, wash in several changes of tepid water to which a little oil has been added. The oil residue clinging to the leaves makes it unnecessary to add any more to the soup.

> $^1/_2$ pound slippery vegetable (*saan choy*)
> $^1/_2$ pound boneless, skinless chicken breasts
> 1 quart unsalted or low-sodium chicken stock
> 1 slice fresh ginger
> 1 teaspoon thin soy sauce
> $^1/_4$ teaspoon black pepper
> 1 scallion, green and white parts minced
> $^1/_4$ cup loosely packed cilantro leaves
> Salt
> 1 large egg, lightly beaten

Wash the slippery vegetable and cut into manageable pieces. Slice the chicken into thin strips.

In a saucepan, heat the stock with the ginger. Simmer 15 to 20 minutes, until flavored. Remove the ginger and discard.

Bring the stock to a gentle boil. Add the chicken and stir with a fork or chopsticks to separate the pieces. When the chicken just turns white, add the slippery vegetable, soy sauce, and pepper. Simmer 10 to 15 minutes, until soft. Add the scallion and cilantro. Season to taste with salt, if necessary. Remove from heat and immediately stir in the beaten egg with a fork. Serve.

Chinese Boxthorn
Gau Gei Choy · Gou Qi Cai
Lycium barbarum (L. chinense)

枸杞菜

The Chinese consider food and health to be closely related. When we were growing up in Hong Kong, sometimes we would arrive at dinner and be given something, most often a soup, which we had to eat as a tonic because of its health-giving properties. I remember our amah standing behind the naughty child—which could be any one of us— threatening a spanking, while she forced down every last drop.

Of course the tonic was not always awful. In the summer, we often had to drink barley water, which was served cold, sweetened, with a bit of lemon added. It was a great favorite with all of us. Soup made with boxthorn and pig's liver was considered a great energizing tonic, especially for me with my nearsighted eyes. I liked the slightly bitter taste and never fussed, although I don't think that all my brothers and sisters cared for it.

I still like boxthorn, also called matrimony vine, not only as a vegetable in soups but because it is so pretty. The long, stiff stems measure 10 to 12 inches, and are covered with bright green oval leaves about 1 inch long. Like common boxwood, sprigs of this vine make a pretty green filler in a flower arrangement. *Gau gei choy* has a slightly bitter taste, not unlike watercress. Perhaps it is this bitterness that has contributed to its medicinal properties.

How to Use
Only the leaves of the boxthorn are used. Check for thorns before stripping leaves. Wash briefly before cooking in soup, usually with pork and pork liver. Boxthorn is available in late spring or early summer, and sometimes in the fall.

Storage and Care
The leaves are delicate, so use boxthorn within a day or two. Store in vegetable bin of refrigerator and wash just prior to use.

Cultivation Tips
Chinese boxthorn is a trailing shrub. It should be propagated by cuttings, but because of its invasive nature, it is not recommended for the home gardener.

Yields 8 servings

The Chinese believe that boxthorn and pork liver soup is good for the eyes. Because I am extremely nearsighted, I make this soup frequently. The liver imparts a slight bitter flavor, which I find interesting. If you prefer you can make this soup with sliced lean pork. Be careful when pinching the leaves off the woody stems, because there are thorns that may prick you badly.

$^3/_4$ pound boxthorn (*gau gei choy*)
1 tablespoon vegetable oil
1 pound pork liver or lean pork, sliced into thin strips
1 scallion, green and white parts minced
1 teaspoon minced fresh ginger
6 cups water or unsalted or low-sodium chicken stock
2 teaspoons thin soy sauce
3 tablespoons sherry
$^1/_2$ teaspoon salt
$^1/_4$ teaspoon black pepper

Pick the leaves off the boxthorn branches, being careful not to prick your fingers on the thorns. You should have about $4^1/_2$ cups of tightly packed leaves. Wash well and drain. Set aside.

In a saucepan or wok, heat the oil over high heat and sauté the liver slices, if using, until lightly browned, about 2 minutes. Remove to a plate and reserve. Add the scallion and ginger, and stir-fry for 10 seconds. Add the water or stock, soy sauce, sherry, and boxthorn leaves. If using pork instead of liver, add also. Simmer 5 minutes (or 20 minutes if using pork slices). Add the salt and pepper, then return the liver, if using, to the soup and cook, covered, 2 to 3 minutes longer. Serve.

Stem Lettuce
Wo Sun · Wo Sun
Lactuca sativa var. *asparagina* (var. *augustana*)

Because the Chinese seldom eat vegetables raw but love the taste of fresh lettuce, stem lettuce is perfect for them. It is a Chinese lettuce cultivated for its stem, and, as its Latin name implies, it looks like a giant asparagus spear with a bunch of leaves at the top of the stem. It never forms a head as some other lettuces do. I have seldom encountered this lettuce in Asian markets in New York, but it is more widely available in California. The seeds are listed by the misleading name celtuce in catalogs. Stem lettuce, also called asparagus lettuce, is a true lettuce, not a hybrid of celery and lettuce. As with all lettuces, it is quite easily cultivated.

Stem lettuce (*wo sun*) is easily recognized by its long thick stem, usually 10 to 12 inches long and 1 to 3 inches thick. The greenish-white stem is marked with scars where leaves have fallen off, and only a small tuft of oval leaves remains at the top. Stem lettuce tastes like a mild lettuce, but has a fresh crisp texture. I think that one day we will be able to find it in abundance here. One reason it has not been widely marketed might be that the Chinese use this vegetable most often to make pickles.

How to Use
Leaves and stems are edible. The stems are usually peeled, cut into matchsticks or small cubes, and then stir-fried lightly and quickly. Stem lettuce can be used on its own, in sauces, or with meat, fish, seafood, or poultry. It is also used in soups or lightly boiled. You can pickle stem lettuce very simply with rice vinegar. Tender young stems and leaves may also be eaten raw.

Storage and Care
As with all vegetables, look for unblemished, firm stems with crisp leaves. Store refrigerated, and wash leaves only when ready to use. Stems should be peeled before using.

Cultivation Tips
Stem lettuce is an annual. It grows in a wide range of temperatures and can withstand light frosts as well as temperatures in the 80s. It grows best in fertile, well-drained soil and should be sown in summer for an autumn crop, or in very hot climates in autumn for a winter

crop. Plants are ready for harvesting in about 85 days and should not be allowed to get too mature, because they become bitter with age.

Stem Lettuce and Chicken

Yields 2 servings

This lettuce is very hard to find in Asian markets outside of California. If you see it, do try it. You can substitute asparagus, but it lacks the delicate flavor of this lettuce.

> 1 stalk stem lettuce (*wo sun*)
> ½ pound boneless, skinless chicken breasts
>
> FOR THE CHICKEN:
> 1 tablespoon thin soy sauce
> 2 teaspoons cornstarch
> 2 teaspoons white wine
>
> •
>
> 1 tablespoon vegetable oil
> 1 teaspoon minced fresh ginger
> 1 teaspoon salt
> ½ teaspoon freshly ground black pepper
> ¼ teaspoon sugar
> 2 tablespoons unsalted or low-sodium chicken stock
> 1 teaspoon roasted sesame oil

Rinse the lettuce and cut the leaves off and reserve. Cut the stem into matchstick-size pieces. Set aside.

Thinly slice the chicken and mix with the soy sauce, cornstarch, and wine. Let stand 10 minutes.

In a wok, heat the oil and stir-fry the ginger 10 seconds or until aromatic. Add the chicken and stir-fry until white, about 5 minutes. Add the matchstick pieces of stem lettuce and stir-fry 1 to 2 minutes, until tender. Add the leaves and continue to stir-fry until wilted. Season with salt, pepper, and sugar. Then add the stock and stir to make a little sauce. Turn off heat and drizzle with sesame oil before serving.

Watercress
Sai Yeung Choy · Xi Yang Cai
Rorippa nasturtium–aquaticum (Nasturtium officinale)

In a culture where nightsoil was used as a fertilizer, eating raw vegetables was uncommon in Hong Kong when I was growing up. We seldom ate raw vegetable salads, and never raw watercress, which was almost always cooked in soups. That is still the way I like it best.

When I started to teach cooking in New York, I was happy to find fresh bunches of watercress available in Chinatown year-round—on the coldest winter day or the hottest summer one. In my very first cooking class, I made a watercress and fish soup. This soup is so easy to make that a cook would include it in a meal almost as an afterthought. I was quite taken aback—and pleasantly surprised—to find how much my students loved this simple, everyday dish. The stronger flavor of cooked watercress was a new taste experience for them.

Watercress was introduced to China by Europeans fairly late, around the end of the nineteenth century. The Chinese embraced it enthusiastically, but preferred it cooked. They love the slightly bitter flavor and mustardy bite, mellowed by cooking, that it gives to soups. In China, a soup is served at every family meal, and watercress— which is rich in iodine, sulphur, iron, potassium, and vitamin C— makes a perfect healthy addition. It is rich in oxalic acid, which helps it to stay bright green when not overcooked. It is available year-round and is inexpensive.

How to Use
The Chinese use watercress only in soups, but it is also great raw and can be steamed, stir-fried, or braised. Dishes that include cooked watercress are common in North American Chinese restaurants.

Storage and Care
Buy crisp fresh bunches, because watercress wilts easily and deteriorates rapidly. Optimally, it should be used within a day. Rinse quickly in cold water.

Cultivation Tips
Not feasible for the home gardener.

Yields 1 cup

This sauce is delicious served with a delicate flounder lightly sautéed in butter, or with a poached chicken breast. The sauce's beautiful jade green color and its slight peppery taste is mellowed with cream to make it a food lover's delight—both on the plate and on the palate!

- 2 bunches watercress (*sai yeung choy*), about $\frac{1}{2}$ pound
- $\frac{1}{2}$ cup heavy cream, preferably not ultrapasteurized
- $\frac{1}{4}$ cup unsalted or low-sodium chicken stock or watercress cooking liquid
- 1 tablespoon plus $\frac{1}{2}$ teaspoon salt
- $\frac{1}{8}$ teaspoon freshly ground black pepper

Wash the watercress and remove the leaves and the stems. Discard the stems. In a saucepan over medium heat, reduce the cream by half, to $\frac{1}{4}$ cup.

Bring a large pot of water to a boil, add 1 tablespoon salt, and quickly blanch the watercress. Prepare a large bowl of ice water. As soon as the watercress turns bright green, drain and plunge into the ice water immediately. If you like, reserve some of the watercress cooking liquid for the sauce. When the leaves are completely cold, drain in a colander, and squeeze slightly to remove excess water.

Puree the watercress thoroughly in a blender, scraping down the sides frequently, about 5 minutes. The result should be a smooth paste.

Add the watercress puree to the reduced cream. Thin with stock or water, and season with salt and pepper. Stir well to blend. If you want to hold the sauce, do not add cream.

Note: If you want to prepare the sauce in advance, stop before you put in the cream. Add the cream just before serving.

2

Gourds·
Melons &
Squashes

Winter Melon
Tung Qwa · Dong Gua
Benincasa hispida

冬
瓜

At least once a year in my family, we would arrive at the dinner table and be presented with a wonderful surprise: *tung qwa chung*, or winter melon pond. Preparing and cooking this dish was quite a feat, so it was always a festive dinner.

The large basketball-size round melon called *tung qwa* is sliced at one end for a lid, the seeds and fibers are taken out, and usually some ornate characters or pictures are carved on the hard, green outer skin, because the shell serves as the container for the soup. Then the melon shell is placed in a sling, made with a large dishtowel, and lowered into a large, shallow bowl sitting on a rack in a giant pot. The melon is then filled with rich chicken stock, strips of ham, chicken, pork, gingko nuts, slivered shiitake mushrooms, and orange peel, and the melon lid is replaced. The melon is steamed for several hours, until the melon flesh is tender and the soup is rich and flavorful. At the last moment, shiny cellophane noodles, or bean threads, are added to the soup. The melon pond is lifted by the sling, transferred to a large, shallow tureen, and brought to the table. If dinner is just a family meal, the winter melon pond is the only dish served. Pieces of the delicious pale green melon are scooped out and served with white rice, and a little of the broth and meat is poured over for a warming dinner. Then more soup is served and the melon scooped out until all that is left is a sagging, deflated squash. At a more formal dinner, other dishes might be served as well, but the melon pond is always the star!

For everyday meals, however, winter melon is more often used as an ingredient in the soup. It is commonly sold by the slice, as even smaller melons usually weigh about 10 pounds. The melon can also be pickled, and is even found cut into cubes and candied, a sweet that is popular at Chinese New Year.

Winter melon is easily recognized by its large round size, hard green skin, and white flesh. Melons are usually 15 inches in diameter and weigh about 12 pounds, although they can reach 20 inches and weigh 60 to 100 pounds. The white flesh has the texture of watermelon, and indeed is more than 95 percent water. The hard, thin dark green skin has a waxy, whitish finish, which explains its other common name of wax gourd. "Winter melon" is a misnomer, as this is really a summer vegetable and requires about five months of warm weather, with temperatures in the seventies, to reach maturity.

However, winter melons do have amazing keeping qualities and have been known to last, properly stored in a cool shed, up to a year.

Although this giant melon has a subtle, rather bland taste, it has been nourishing Asians for centuries. Prized by the Chinese for its refreshing qualities in summer soups, it is often also prepared with barley, lotus seeds, and herbs as a tonic soup.

How to Use

For everyday use, buy winter melon in firm, white slices. Peel off the coarse green skin and remove any seeds and fibrous inner core. Cut into large cubes or sticks. Although it is possible to stir-fry, braise, or steam this melon, the taste and texture do not contribute to a superior dish. The melon is best used in soups, seasoned strongly.

Storage and Care

If buying a whole melon, look for smaller ones, as they are stronger in flavor and easier to handle. Whole melons should be firm and have a waxy finish. Melon slices should have clean-looking and firm white flesh. Smell the melon to be sure it has not picked up any odors. Whole melons will keep at a cool room temperature (about 50 degrees) for months, but melon slices should be used within a day of purchase, as they deteriorate rapidly.

Cultivation Tips

Not recommended for the home gardener. This annual needs a lot of space, a long summer, and continual care. Setting fruit may be difficult and hand pollination is often necessary.

Winter Melon-Squab Soup

Yields 4 servings

Preparing a whole winter melon for soup is quite an undertaking, and many recipes already exist. Commonly, you can buy slices of winter melon, and this recipe uses sliced melon. The squab and ham in the soup give it a luxurious richness that defines this as a special or banquet dish, despite the ease with which it can be prepared.

    2 squab, about 1 pound each
    1 tablespoon dark soy sauce
    3 cups unsalted or low-sodium chicken stock
    1 slice fresh ginger
    1 scallion, trimmed
    1 1/2-pound slice winter melon (*tung qwa*)
    1 tablespoon vegetable oil
    4 ounces Westphalian ham or prosciutto

2-inch by ¹/₂-inch piece of orange peel
1 tablespoon dry sherry
Zest of 1 orange (optional)

With a sharp knife, remove the necks and wing tips of the squab. Remove the gizzards and livers; discard livers or save for another use. Cut the squab in half lengthwise, rub inside and out with soy sauce, and set aside.

In a saucepan, bring the chicken stock, squab parts and gizzards, ginger, and scallion to a simmer. Simmer 30 minutes to flavor. Strain the stock and set aside.

Peel the melon and remove the seeds and stringy parts. Slice into 2-inch-thick pieces. Arrange in the bottom of a deep pot in one or more rows.

In a wok, heat the oil and brown the squab halves. Arrange in the pot alongside the melon, skin side out. Roll up the ham slices and cut into 1-inch-thick ribbons. Scatter over the melon and squab.

Gently pour the flavored stock into the pot, add the orange peel and sherry, and simmer gently for 1 hour, or until soup tastes rich and slightly smoky.

To serve, place each squab half in a deep bowl together with a few melon pieces and spoon in the broth. Garnish with orange zest, if desired.

Fuzzy Melon
Mo Qwa, Tseet Qwa · Mao Gua, Jie Gua
Benincasa hispida var. *chieh-qua*

In our house, every child was expected to appear at the dinner table on time, faces and hands washed and reasonably neatly dressed. During the hot, humid days of a Hong Kong summer, when we were on school vacation, this was a bit of a drag, as we would linger outside to play and then often race home just in time to get to the table—or risk being punished if we were late. It was often too hot to eat very much, but I remember eagerly anticipating a bowl of fuzzy melon soup. It was generally held that in very hot weather, drinking something hot was more refreshing than having an ice-cold drink, so this was a standby in summer. I still enjoy fuzzy melon soup on a hot summer day.

The light broth is enriched with strips of pork or ham, and in addition to the chunks of watery melon, there are silvery strands of cellophane, or bean thread, noodles. We were scolded if we slurped the noddles noisily, but reprimands could not deter us from enjoying this delicious soup, and only encouraged giggles and laughter.

Fuzzy or hairy melons are a form of winter melon. When young they have a covering of soft downy hairs that disappears in the mature fruit. The melons are shaped like a slightly waisted cucumber, but are much larger and have a splotchy green color. They usually measure 6 to 10 inches long and about 2 inches in diameter. They are firmer in texture than watermelon or winter melon, and have a subtle flavor like most summer squashes.

How to Use
Abundantly available, particularly in warm months, fuzzy melon should be peeled—or scrubbed if used unpeeled. The melon can be shredded, cubed, sliced, or stuffed. Very popular in soup, the flesh can also be steamed, boiled, braised, stir-fried, pickled, candied, and even shredded and eaten raw. Because its flavor is bland, it absorbs flavors well and is good stir-fried with meat or seafood in a strong-tasting sauce, such as oyster sauce.

Storage and Care
Fuzzy melon should be stored in the vegetable bin of the refrigerator, just like zucchini. Placing it in a paper bag will improve its keeping qualities, but the melon should last about a week if it hasn't been sitting in the store a long time already. It should be firm and unblemished, without dark spots.

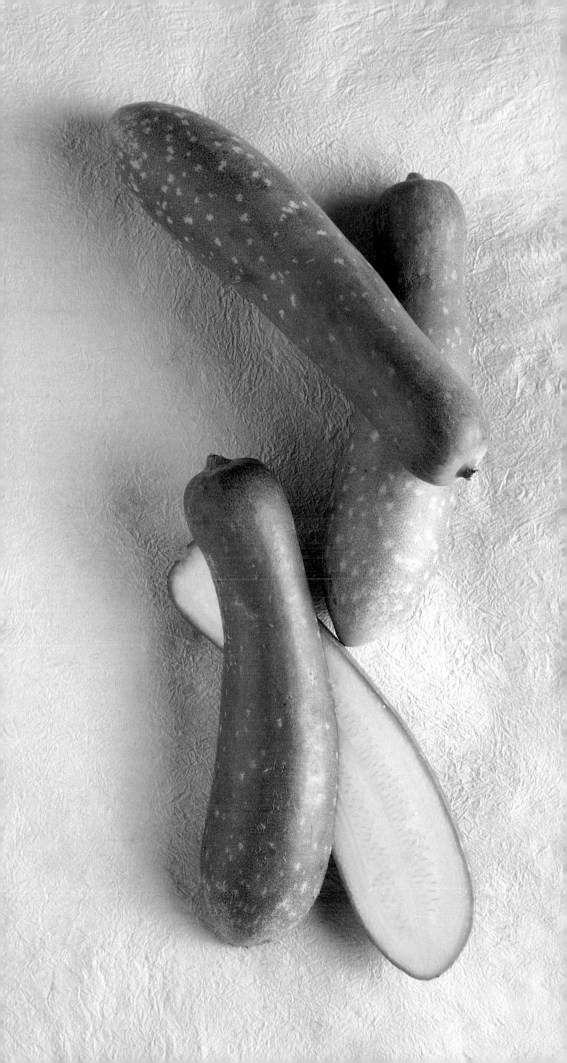

Cultivation Tips

Although the vines of fuzzy melon are more compact than winter melon vines, they need to be supported. The melons require three months to mature, but as for winter melon, pollination is tricky. I do not recommend growing this annual unless you are a most avid and experienced home gardener.

Fuzzy Melon Soup

Yields: 6 to 8 servings

The lemongrass broth and Chinese celery (see page 165) give this soup a special flavor, but it will still taste good if you use chicken stock and regular branch celery. Just use twice as much branch celery as the Chinese kind because of its gentler flavor.

> 2 fuzzy melons (*mo qwa*), about 1¾ to 2 pounds
> 2 ounces cellophane noodles (bean threads)
> 1 teaspoon vegetable oil
> 1 scallion, green and white parts minced
> 1 tablespoon minced Chinese celery (*kun choy*)
> 4 cups Lemongrass Broth (page 168)
> 1 teaspoon thin soy sauce
> ½ teaspoon Japanese pepper (see Note)

Peel and halve the melons. Remove the seeds and stringy insides. Cut into 2-inch pieces. Soak noodles in warm water until soft and pliable, 10 to 15 minutes. Drain and set aside. Noodles can be cut into 4-inch lengths for easier serving, but Asians never do this!

In a saucepan, heat the oil and lightly sauté the scallion and celery until aromatic, about 30 seconds. Add the melon pieces, broth, soy sauce, and pepper and bring to a boil. Reduce heat and simmer 20 to 30 minutes, until the melon is tender. Add the drained noodles, stir, and cook 1 minute. Serve.

Note: Sansho, commonly labeled as Japanese pepper, is available in stores that sell Japanese foods. Or use Szechuan pepper, which is closely related.

Bitter Melon
Fu Qwa · Ku Gua
Momordica charantia

苦
瓜

This melon illustrates perfectly the Chinese love of bitter flavors. Although little known in the West, bitter melon is appreciated for its bitter taste throughout Asia. It is widely used in Indonesia, India, Sri Lanka, and the Philippines. On a visit to any Asian market or Chinatown, you will easily recognize bitter melon by its warty appearance. The vegetable is usually 6 to 10 inches long, shaped like a cucumber. The best ones are pale green: dark green indicates an immature melon that is too bitter; an overripe melon is orange and too sweet and soft.

How to Use
Bitter melon can be stewed, steamed, braised, curried, and stir-fried. It is also pickled and used to make chutney. The bitter taste is caused by the presence of quinine, *qwing*, so this melon has medicinal qualities as well. After washing well, halve the unpeeled melon lengthwise and discard the seeds and woody inner core. Blanch in boiling water 2 to 3 minutes, until it turns bright green. Drain, plunge in cold water to refresh, and use as desired. To decrease the bitterness, salt the halved or sliced unpeeled melon liberally, let stand for 10 to 15 minutes, then rinse and squeeze dry before using.

Bitter melon's sharp flavor softens as it absorbs other flavors, so Chinese cooks like to flavor *fu qwa* dishes with strong flavors, such as black beans. In stir-fries, it blends well with pork, beef, and chicken.

Storage and Care
Buy young pale green melons that are firm and unblemished. They can be kept unwashed in the vegetable bin of the refrigerator for up to one week. Wash well before using, but do not peel. Remove seeds and soft woody centers.

Cultivating Tips
Bitter melon is recommended only for very experienced gardeners who live in hot, humid areas. The plant thrives in almost any kind of soil, but needs plenty of water. Gardeners in temperate zones may find this plant too troublesome to be worth cultivating.

The seeds should be soaked overnight in water, as germination can be a problem. They can then be sown in pots and transplanted outdoors after the temperature does not fall below 50°F. Germination

should occur between five days and one week. In very hot areas, seeds can be sown directly where they will grow. The vines need to be trained on a trellis, to allow fruit, which matures in about 80 days, to hang down. The vines need to be cut back if they become too bushy.

Bitter Melon with Sliced Chicken

Yields 4 servings

I love bitter melon so much that I was surprised when I couldn't get my friends and recipe testers, Whitney Clay and Clayton Cooke, to like this dish! After one taste, both of them said it was definitely an "acquired taste." But perhaps you will take to this classic Asian dish.

1 pound boneless, skinless chicken breasts

FOR THE CHICKEN:
1 tablespoon thin soy sauce
1 tablespoon dry sherry
1 teaspoon cornstarch

1 bitter melon (*fu qwa*), about $1/2$ to $3/4$ pound
1 tablespoon baking soda
2 tablespoons fermented black beans
2 tablespoons vegetable oil
2 garlic cloves, minced
2 teaspoons minced fresh ginger
1 scallion, green and white parts minced
2 teaspoons thin soy sauce
$1/4$ cup cold water, mixed with 1 tablespoon cornstarch

Slice the chicken thinly and combine with the soy sauce, sherry, and cornstarch. Let stand 10 minutes or longer.

Cut the unpeeled melon in half, and with a spoon, scrape away seeds and woody core. Bring a pot of water to a boil, add the baking soda, and blanch the melon for a minute or two, until the skin turns bright jade green. This removes some of the bitter taste. Drain and refresh in ice water. When the melon is cold, remove from the water and slice into half-moon shapes about $1/4$ inch thick.

Soak the black beans in warm water until soft, about 2 minutes, drain, and mash slightly.

In a wok, heat the oil, then add the garlic, ginger, scallion, and black beans. Stir-fry 30 seconds, then add the chicken and cook, tossing, until the chicken turns white, about 5 minutes. Add the melon and continue to stir-fry 2 to 3 minutes, or until the melon is hot. Add the soy sauce and cornstarch mixture. Bring to a boil, stirring until sauce thickens. Serve over white rice.

Chinese Eggplant
Ai Qwa · Ai Gua
Solanum melongena

Eggplant lovers are always excited to discover new varieties of their favorite vegetable, be it the round white eggplant, the baby eggplant, or the elegant Chinese eggplant. Chinese eggplants range in color from pale mauve to deep purple; they have few if any seeds and a thin skin. They are also known as Japanese eggplants.

Eggplants are thought to have originated in India and been introduced via Southeast Asia to China, where they have been cultivated since 600 B.C. Eggplant did not reach western Europe until about the twelfth century, but eggplant dishes have been made famous by the Greeks, Italians, Spanish, and French. I believe that the Chinese love eggplant for its texture; as it does not have too strong a flavor, they tend to prepare it with strong-tasting ingredients.

Chinese eggplants are long and slim, about 2 inches thick and 6 to 10 inches long. In some Asian markets it is also possible to find the tiny, round pea eggplant (*Solanum torvum*). When I first saw this vegetable, I mistook the tiny fruit for the tomatillos used in Mexican cooking. The pea eggplant is used mainly in Thai cooking. It is about the size of a cherry tomato, but is usually pale to dark green, and sometimes almost white. Pea eggplants have a sour flavor, are hard because they are unripe, and are usually ground up with other ingredients for chutneys, curries, and sauces.

Eggplant is not particularly nutritious, but it is low in calories if not deep-fried or cooked in too much oil. It blends well with many strong flavors. Unlike other vegetables popular in Chinese cooking, eggplant is best cooked by itself or with other vegetables. It does not go well in stir-fries with meat, poultry, or fish.

How to Use
Buy firm, unblemished eggplants. They can be used peeled or unpeeled. Slice or cut to desired size. Salting the eggplant before use draws out excess moisture and a slight bitter taste; the salt is then rinsed off before cooking. Eggplant can be baked, fried, stir-fried, batter-fried, used in tempura, or braised—served hot or cold.

Storage and Care
If firm, eggplant keeps one week to ten days, refrigerated. Brown soft spots appear as the vegetable ages.

Cultivation Tips

Recommended for most gardeners. Eggplant will not flourish until temperatures have settled and remain in the high 70s. Seed should be sown indoors, eight weeks prior to transplanting. For gardeners in cooler zones, several catalogs offer early-producing varieties. The plants should be pruned and staked. Harvest the fruits when they reach a usable size, leaving one or two to encourage more fruit.

Chinese Eggplant Relish

Yields about 1 quart

At first I wanted to make a chutney, but Chinese eggplants hold their shape so well during cooking that the jamlike consistency of a chutney is difficult to achieve. But the result is nonetheless delicious, so I call this a relish and have learned something new about eggplants.

> 1 pound Chinese eggplant (*ai qwa*)
> 1 tablespoon plus 1 teaspoon Kosher salt
> $^1/_2$ cup raisins
> 1 tablespoon vegetable oil
> 1 Vidalia or other sweet onion (about $^1/_2$ pound), coarsely chopped
> 1 teaspoon minced fresh ginger
> 1 garlic clove, minced
> 2 hot red or green chilies
> $^1/_4$ cup rice vinegar
> $^1/_4$ cup sugar
> $^1/_4$ teaspoon ground cumin
> $^1/_4$ teaspoon ground coriander
> $^1/_4$ teaspoon turmeric
> $^1/_8$ teaspoon ground allspice
> 2 tablespoons lemon juice

Wash the eggplant and cut it into slices about $^1/_2$ inch thick. Set in a colander and sprinkle with 1 tablespoon salt. Let stand in the sink about 30 minutes. Meanwhile, cover the raisins with hot water to plump them. Let stand 15 to 30 minutes, then drain. Rinse off salt from eggplant slices and pat dry with paper towels.

In a skillet, heat the oil and sauté the onion until wilted, stirring to prevent burning. Add the eggplant and stir while cooking, about 3 to 5 minutes. Add the raisins, ginger, garlic, chilies, remaining 1 teaspoon salt, vinegar, sugar, cumin, coriander, turmeric, allspice, lemon juice, and $^1/_2$ cup water. Bring to a simmer and cook 30 to 40 minutes, stirring often. If mixture gets too dry, add a little more water. Serve at room temperature.

Angled Luffa, Smooth Luffa
Sze Qwa, Seui Qwa · Si Gua, Shui Gua
Luffa acutangula, Luffa cylindrica

My favorite soup as a child was a clear broth with roll-cut pieces of angled luffa and cellophane noodles, or bean threads. There was something about the pale green pieces of slightly spongy squash and the transparent noodles that I found enchanting. Luffa squash has a flavor reminiscent of zucchini flowers, a slightly spongy texture, and a sweet juiciness. Actually, calling this vegetable a squash is not quite correct—it is really a gourd.

There are two varieties of luffa: angled (or silk squash) and smooth (or sponge). Luffa grown as a vegetable should be harvested when immature, as older fruits become bitter and develop purgative qualities. The angled luffa is more commonly marketed and preferred, although both varieties of the young fruit are edible. Smooth luffa is grown to maturity and dried for use as a bath scrubber, and in China dried luffa scrubbers are also used in the kitchen, much as we use steel wool.

You will easily recognize angled luffa by its dark green color and the ridges that run down the length of the squash. It is usually 8 to 10 inches long and about 2 to 3 inches thick, with a slight curve. I like to test for freshness by taking hold of one end and gently waving it back and forth. If it is fresh, it will not break easily.

Although not so common, you will be able to identify smooth luffa by its larger, cylindrical shape, with a slight thickening toward the bottom of the fruit, so that it resembles a bat. It usually measures 12 to 18 inches long and is much heavier than angled luffa. Sometimes there may be a very slight ridge or stripe, and the green is lighter. At present, I have rarely seen this in markets in New York's Chinatown.

How to Use
Scrub the luffa and peel only the ridges—or completely, if the skin is tough. Cut into pieces using the roll-cut technique, or slice as desired. Luffa can also be peeled and grated. Angled luffa can be used in soups, stir-fried, sautéed, braised by itself, or cooked with meats. If you grow this plant in your garden, the leaves and tender shoots are also edible and can be stir-fried and used like any other leafy green.

Storage and Care
Luffa will keep in the vegetable bin of the refrigerator two to five days if very fresh. They will become mushy and moldy as they age or if

allowed to get too moist. Luffa is best used within a day or so of purchase.

Cultivation Tips

I do not recommend growing luffas, except for the most avid and expert gardeners with large gardens in tropical climates. They need lots of room and long, hot, sunny days. Choose a well-prepared site enriched with compost and manure, and give plenty of water and good drainage. Seeds should be soaked overnight before planting. When plants are 3 to 5 inches high, begin to train them on a trellis, so the fruit will hang down. Fruit will not be ready for harvesting for two to three months; pick when 6 to 8 inches long if used as a vegetable.

An interesting exercise for the ambitious gardener might be to leave the smooth luffas to mature and begin to wither. They can then be picked, peeled, and the seed and pulp removed, then left to dry. When completely dried, they are then soaked, bleached if desired, and used for the bath.

Angled Luffa Squash Sauté

Yields 2 servings

Although this squash is most often cooked in a clear soup, I find that the delicate flavor comes through very well when sautéed this way.

> 2 angled luffa squash (*sze qwa*), about ¾ to 1 pound
> 2 tablespoons butter
> 2 tablespoons minced shallots
> 1 tablespoon minced fresh parsley
> ½ teaspoon salt
> ¼ teaspoon freshly ground black pepper
> Pinch of sugar
> 1 tablespoon grated Parmesan cheese

Peel the squash and slice into 1-inch circles.

In a skillet, heat the butter and sauté the shallots until soft. Add the squash and continue cooking, stirring often, for 5 minutes or until squash is crisp but tender. Add the parsley, salt, pepper, and sugar. Cook, stirring, another minute or two. Turn off the heat and sprinkle with Parmesan cheese before serving.

Angled Luffa

Bottle Gourd
Po Qwa, Woo Lo Qwa · Hu Lu Gua
Lagenaria siceraria

Whenever I see the baseball bat shape of the bottle gourd, called *po qwa* in Cantonese, I remember one of my mother's favorite conserves. I think of the brown earthenware jars that used to hold the jam for breakfast and tea. The *po qwa* was peeled and shredded into long, thin strips, then cooked in syrup until thick. I recall being fascinated with the long shreds, and I would pull them apart as I ate the jam by spoonfuls rather than spreading the jam on bread. Our amah, who was always concerned about our good manners, would reprimand me and hit my hands, saying that this behavior was most unladylike.

There are two common types of bottle gourd, easily differentiated by their shape, although only immature gourds of both varieties are used as a vegetable. The baseball bat-shaped one is *po qwa*, while the distinctive *woo lo qwa* looks like an ewer or bottle—and in fact, the mature fruit develops a hard shell and they can be hollowed out and slowly dried for use as a receptacle. *Woo lo qwa*, with their round bottoms and thin necks, are a favorite subject of ancient Chinese artists.

Bottle gourds have a light green skin and white, smooth-textured flesh with a mild taste much like summer squash. The bottle type usually ranges from 8 inches long and 3 to 5 inches across at its thickest part to the size of a large football, while the bat type can be anywhere from 12 to 30 inches long and 3 to 4 inches thick.

How to Use
Buy fresh, firm gourds. Peel and scoop out the seeds, and cut as desired; or cut in half, remove the seeds, and hollow out slightly, then stuff with a mixture of meat and vegetables and bake. More commonly the gourds are used in soups and stir-fries, and the bottle type can be hollowed out and filled with soup, as with a winter melon. The Japanese dry strips of the gourd to use as the edible ribbon known as *kampyo*.

Storage and Care
Treat bottle gourd as a winter squash. If very fresh, they will keep as long as a month in the refrigerator or a cool room.

Cultivation Tips
While not difficult to grow, bottle gourds require lot of room or need to be trained on trellises, and must be hand-pollinated.

Yields 3 8-ounce jars

I thought it would be nice to make the jam I remembered from my childhood, but I had no idea how to begin. I had a vivid memory of what it should taste like, but I was troubled that the raw gourd had a very subtle flavor. I called my friend Nick Malgieri, the pastry expert, whom I often consult on baking and sweets. Nick was intrigued with the idea and guided me through the stages for this jam. As the squash cooks, its flavor intensifies. The jam is really quite easy to make, especially in relatively small quantities. If you are unsure about canning, simply refrigerate the jars.

> 1 3¼-pound bottle gourd (*po qwa*)
> 2½ cups sugar
> 1 cup light corn syrup
> 3 tablespoons lemon juice

Peel the gourd, cut in half, and seed completely. Grate the gourd with the largest holes of a hand grater, or use a food processor to grate coarsely. You should have about 6 cups. Place the grated gourd in a heavy saucepan, cover with 3 cups cold water, and bring to a boil. Reduce the heat to simmer and cook until the shreds are translucent and tender, about 20 minutes. Strain, reserving 1 cup of the cooking water.

In a heavy saucepan, combine the reserved cooking water, sugar, corn syrup, and lemon juice. Bring to a boil, reduce the heat, and stir to dissolve the sugar. Add the gourd and cook until the mixture reaches gel stage, about 2 hours. To check, a few drops of syrup will run together when dripped from a spoon, or mixture will reach 230°F. on a candy thermometer. Stir frequently to prevent sticking, especially toward the end of cooking time.

Spoon into sterile glass canning jars, and seal and process as per manufacturer's instructions.

Green Papaya
Muk Qwa · Mu Gua

Carica papaya

木
瓜

We are all familiar with papaya as a fruit, but as far as I know only Asians and Pacific Islanders use the immature or green papaya as a vegetable. One of our family's favorite home recipes from Macao was to braise cubes of pork and chunks of green papaya in a sauce flavored with pungent preserved shrimp. The delicate sweetness of the papaya was a great foil for the salty, strong-flavored pork.

The first time I ate green papaya in a restaurant was at a Thai place in Rochester, New York. Imagine my surprise when my host ordered the Thai salad, *som tom*, and I saw mounds of shredded green papaya. As both of us loved spicy food, we had asked that all the dishes be made especially hot, and this was no exception. The cool papaya was perfect in this spicy salad.

You will recognize the bulbous shape of the papaya, also known sometimes as a pawpaw. Most green papayas in Asian markets are larger than the ripe ones found in supermarkets. Sometimes, larger fruit will be slightly more elongated. Sizes and shapes vary, from the familiar bulbous to an elongated football; the fruits can measure from 4 to 5 inches long to as much as 15 inches. The skin ranges from completely dark green to green with blushes of red or orange, depending on the degree of ripeness. Ripe orange or yellow papayas can't be used as a vegetable. Green papayas taste like papaya, but are barely sweet and quite firm. The flesh can be pale green or orange colored, and often will turn rosy after cooking.

How to Use
Green papaya should be peeled, halved, and the seeds scooped out and discarded. Cut the flesh into cubes, slices, or shred as desired. Papaya is good raw, in soups, braised, and, when shredded, in pancakes or fritters.

Storage and Care
Store in a cool room or refrigerate. Depending on ripeness, a green papaya should keep one week to ten days, or longer.

Cultivation Tips
Not recommended for the home gardener.

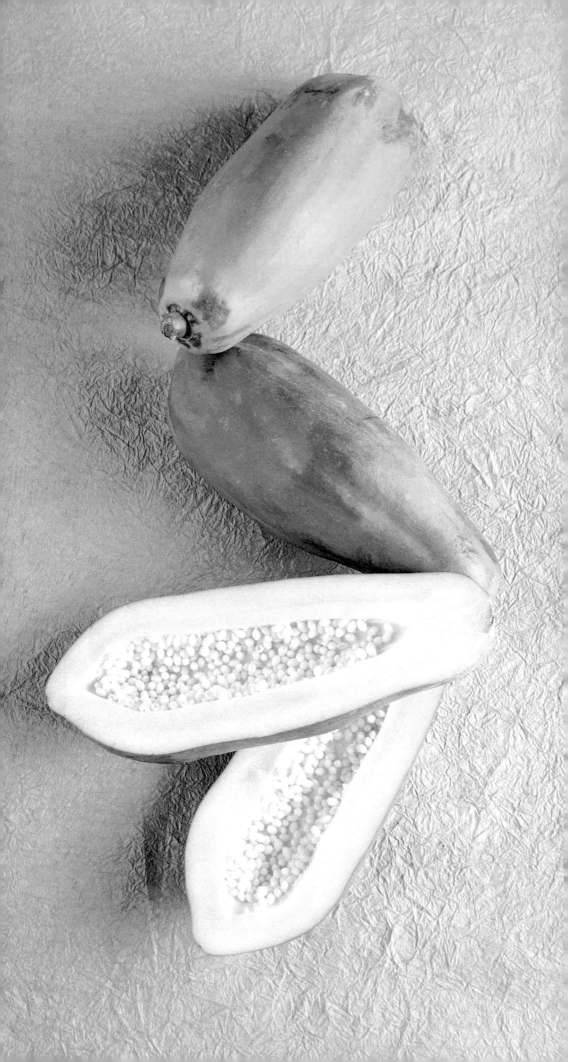

Yields about 36 3-inch pancakes

This recipe was suggested to me by my student Melody Santos, who is from the Philippines. I think these pancakes are delicious, and they make a great appetizer for cocktails. Serve them with a dipping sauce of thin soy sauce mixed with some lemon juice or rice vinegar.

1 green papaya (*muk qwa*), about 2 pounds
8 ounces medium shrimp

FOR THE BATTER:
$\frac{1}{2}$ cup all-purpose flour
$\frac{1}{2}$ cup cornstarch
2 teaspoons salt
1 teaspoon freshly ground black pepper
3 eggs, beaten
2 scallions, green and white parts minced

$\frac{1}{4}$ cup vegetable oil

Peel and cut the papaya in half. Using a spoon, scoop out all the seeds. Shred the papaya with a coarse grater or food processor. There should be about 5 cups packed.

Peel and devein the shrimp and coarsely chop by hand. Set aside.

Make the batter. In a large bowl, stir together the flour, cornstarch, salt, and pepper. Add the beaten eggs and $\frac{1}{2}$ cup cold water and whisk to a smooth batter. Fold in the scallions, papaya shreds, and shrimp. Mix to blend well.

Heat a large, heavy skillet and pour in just enough oil to coat the bottom. Pour in 2 tablespoons of the papaya mix to form a pancake about 3 inches round. Cook 1 to 2 minutes over medium heat, then turn and cook an additional minute or until the pancake is lightly browned. Transfer pancake to a paper-towel lined plate and keep warm. Continue adding oil as needed until all the batter is used up, stirring the batter every now and then to keep it well blended. The pancakes may be reheated in a low oven. Serve hot.

Chayote
Hop Jeung Qwa, Faat Sau Qwa · He Zhang Gua, Fo Shou Gua
Sechium edule

The streets, stalls, and markets of New York City's Chinatown are just like they were in the Hong Kong of my youth—more so than in modern Hong Kong. In the early spring, I sometimes steal a day and wander through Chinatown by myself, with no errand to run and plenty of time. I might pop into the herbal medicine shop and ask for some ginseng or a tonic tea, browse through shops filled with tourist souvenirs, or stop at a vegetable stall for a favorite vegetable, such as chayote.

Although chayote is native to Mexico and Central America, it has been embraced enthusiastically by the Chinese. This pear-shaped vegetable has a mild taste that is not very distinctive, so I can only surmise that it is popular for its shape. The Cantonese name describes the folded hands of a praying Buddha, which has only good connotations.

Chayote is likely to be familiar to many Americans. In the South, it is called mirliton, and in the Caribbean it goes by the romantic name christophine. The pale green vegetable usually measures 4 to 6 inches high and about 3 inches at the base. The skin is smooth, but it has one to five clearly defined ridges that run the length of the fruit.

How to Use
Chayote can be used peeled or unpeeled. The skin is edible if tender, as is the seed, although this may be discarded. Wash and cut as desired. The chayote can be used in soup, braised, and stir-fried with meat, even stuffed. It can also be eaten raw in salads. Although really a gourd, any recipe calling for summer squash would be appropriate for chayote.

Storage and Care
Choose firm, unblemished fruit. Keep in a cool place or in the refrigerator for up to several months.

Cultivation Tips
This perennial vine flourishes in a tropical climate, but will grow back each spring in temperate areas if protected with a deep mulch. The plant is very fast growing; to plant, put the whole fruit in the soil with the broad side down. As with all gourds, chayote needs fertile soil with plenty of organic matter. Do not overwater the young plant, but mature plants need generous waterings to thrive.

Yields 4 to 6 servings

The creamy dressing is a nice counterpoint to the crunchy chayote and snow peas. In addition to being a refreshing salad that is unusual and tasty, the two different color greens of the vegetables present a pretty yin-yang picture on the plate. If you don't have plum wine, you can use sweet port or Madeira.

1 pound chayote (*hop jeung qwa*)
1 tablespoon salt
¼ pound snow peas

FOR THE DRESSING:
3 tablespoons plain yogurt
2 teaspoons grainy mustard
½ garlic clove, smashed and very finely chopped
2 tablespoons plum wine
¼ cup vegetable oil
¼ teaspoon Szechuan peppercorns, toasted and crushed
½ teaspoon salt
1 tablespoon black sesame seeds
½ cup roasted and lightly salted cashews, coarsely chopped

Peel the chayote, cut in half, and remove the seed. Cut in half again and slice thinly.

Bring a pot of water to a boil, add the salt, and blanch the snow peas a few seconds, just until they turn a bright green. Drain and plunge into ice water. When cold, cut the snow peas into slivers. There should be about 1 cup. Toss the chayote and snow peas in a salad bowl.

Make the dressing. In a small bowl, combine the yogurt, mustard, and garlic. Whisk in the wine and oil until smooth and creamy. Add the peppercorns and salt. You may hold the dressing in the refrigerator at this point up to 5 days.

Just before serving, whisk dressing again to blend, if necessary, then fold in sesame seeds and cashews. Pour over salad and serve immediately.

See photograph on pages 64–65.

Winter Squash
Naam Qwa · Nan Gua
Cucurbita moschata

南
瓜

I guess it is inevitable that there is a vegetable that I don't particularly like. The Asian representative of the pumpkin family has never been a favorite, and it is only after I came to America and discovered pumpkin pie that I found a dish I could enjoy.

The term winter squash (*naam qwa*) encompasses all the pumpkinlike squashes grown in Asia, falling into two general categories. The first is the elongated football shape with coarse outer skins ranging in color from dark green, to green brushed with orange or yellow, to tan-colored. They measure 6 to 10 inches in diameter and are 12 to 15 inches long. The second type was originally cultivated in Japan, where it was much more popular than in China. It is a round, flattish pumpkin with dark green, yellowish, or reddish skin. Some of these have a more conical or turban shape and are known as the Hokkaido or turban type. They measure from 6 to 10 inches in diameter and can weigh from 5 to 10 pounds.

Both varieties taste like pumpkin, but are firmer in texture and less watery. They are tender, sweet, and flavorful.

How to Use
Fully mature fruits are best and sweetest. Peel the outer skin and remove the seeds, which are sometimes dried, roasted, salted, and eaten as a snack. Cut and shred as desired. *Naam qwa* may be steamed, braised, stewed, used in soups, batter-coated and deep-fried in tempura, and even hollowed out and used as a receptacle for steamed foods.

Storage and Care
As with all winter squashes, these keep very well. Stored in a cool, dry environment, they should keep several months.

Cultivation Tips
Although not difficult to grow and relatively pest resistant, winter squash is a vine that requires a lot of space and the fruits are not ready to harvest for three to four months.

Yields 10 servings

I thought that in a book on vegetables it would be interesting to have one or two sweet recipes, so I decided to include this cake. The texture of the squash is much like pumpkin, but not as watery. You will find this cake moist, so it keeps well. Buy a whole small squash or a large section of a large one.

> 1 small squash or large section of winter squash (*naam qwa*), about 1½ pounds
> 2 teaspoons grated fresh ginger
> 1½ cups all-purpose flour
> 1 teaspoon baking soda
> ½ teaspoon salt
> ½ teaspoon ground cardamom
> ½ teaspoon ground cinnamon
> ½ teaspoon freshly grated nutmeg
> ½ teaspoon ground allspice
> ½ cup vegetable oil
> ½ cup buttermilk
> 3 eggs
> 1 cup granulated sugar
> 1 tablespoon butter, to grease pan
> Confectioners' sugar, for dusting cake

Preheat the oven to 375°F. Generously grease and flour a 10-inch tube pan or Bundt pan.

Peel and seed the squash and grate by hand or in a food processor. You should have 4 cups packed grated squash. Toss with grated ginger, then set aside.

Sift together the flour, baking soda, salt, cardamom, cinnamon, nutmeg, and allspice.

In a large bowl, whisk together the oil, buttermilk, eggs, and sugar; whisk until sugar is almost completely dissolved. Gradually whisk in the flour mixture to form a smooth batter, then fold in the squash and ginger. Mix to blend well. Pour the batter into prepared pan and bake 40 to 50 minutes, until a thin skewer inserted at the center comes out clean.

Cool cake on a rack in pan for 15 minutes. Unmold cake and cool completely. Dust with confectioners' sugar before serving.

Roots· Rhizomes· Corms & Tubers

Stem Ginger, Common Ginger
Tsee Geung, Geung · Zi Jiang, Jiang
Zingiber officinale

Ginger has been prized since ancient times for its medicinal and spiritual properties. It was found in the famous Han tomb excavated in 1972, buried with a noble lady twenty-one centuries ago. Fresh ginger gives Chinese food its characteristic flavor. Powdered ginger is not a good substitute.

When I started to teach cooking, and I would specify to my students just one slice of ginger, they would look skeptical, questioning whether this was really enough. But on tasting the finished dish—say, a whole poached chicken that had been cooked in a large pot of water flavored with only one or two small slices of ginger—they began to realize just how important ginger was in Chinese cooking: the whole chicken was permeated with a ginger flavor.

Fresh mature ginger is a rhizome that is harvested when the ginger plant is seven to ten months old and the leaves have yellowed and died back. Large pieces come in handlike formations, but these are often broken into knobby lengths of different sizes. Ginger knobs usually measure $1\frac{1}{2}$ to 2 inches thick, can be anywhere from 4 to 8 inches long, and are covered with a thin, shiny, light brown skin. The flesh of the ginger is pale yellow and juicy. Older ginger tends to be fibrous. Although I don't always peel ginger before use in everyday dishes, it is easily peeled with a vegetable peeler or can be scraped with the blade of a small knife (or, for fun, the squared end of a Chinese chopstick). The volatile oil in ginger creates its strong aroma, while the oleoresin gives it pungency. As the pieces of ginger age, they become wrinkled and dry.

Besides mature ginger, in Asian markets you will also find young ginger, or stem ginger, harvested when it is three to four months old, before any skin has formed. Young ginger is smooth and ivory colored, with rosy tips where the stems are developing. It has the same shape as mature ginger, but is much more fragrant, juicy, and pungent, with a crisp texture. Stem ginger is much loved by Asians, who often use it abundantly in stir-fried dishes as they would a vegetable.

Purists specify that only stem ginger should be used for authentic ginger beef. Although ginger is available year-round, stem ginger is seasonal. It can be found in early spring through to early summer, and again in the early fall.

Stem Ginger

How to Use

Mature ginger can be used peeled or unpeeled, shredded, minced, and in slices. A little goes a long way. Stem ginger can be candied, pickled, or used as a vegetable or seasoning. Although it is juicy and quite pungent, stem ginger is not as spicy as mature ginger.

Storage and Care

Mature ginger, when used often, can be left unwrapped in the vegetable bin of the refrigerator. It will keep for months if not allowed to get moist. Stem ginger is best used within a few days, as it is more tender and perishable.

For longer storage of both types, submerge the ginger in a container of sherry or dry white wine. Cut off pieces and use as desired; as a bonus, you can use the sherry or wine, which will acquire an intense ginger flavor, for cooking or drinking.

Cultivation Tips

Ginger is not a practical plant for home gardeners.

Ginger Broth

Yields 1 quart

I often use ginger broth in recipes to enhance the taste without adding fresh ginger, which can be a bit too sharp.

> 1 quart homemade chicken stock, degreased
> 1 1-ounce piece fresh ginger (*geung*), thinly sliced and slivered

In a stockpot, bring the stock and ginger to a boil. Reduce the heat to low and gently simmer the broth for 20 minutes. Turn off the heat and let stand until cool, at least 30 minutes. Strain and discard the ginger. Store in the refrigerator for up to 3 to 5 days.

Ginger Caramel Sauce

Yields approximately 1½ cups

This gingery sauce is great with Sweet Potato Pudding (page 121), but it is also super on vanilla ice cream. Make a double batch and keep it handy in the refrigerator.

> 1⅓ cups heavy cream
> ¼ cup slivered fresh ginger (*geung*)
>
> FOR THE CARAMEL:
> 1 cup sugar
> ⅛ teaspoon cream of tartar

In a heavy saucepan, combine the cream and ginger. Bring to a simmer over low heat and cook 15 minutes, or until the cream has a strong ginger flavor. The cream will reduce by about half. Strain out the ginger and discard. Let the cream cool slightly, but do not let it get completely cold.

Meanwhile, make the caramel. Combine 1/3 cup water with the sugar and cream of tartar in a heavy saucepan. Bring to a boil, reduce heat to medium, and stir to dissolve sugar. Continue to cook sugar syrup, brushing down the sides of the pot with a pastry brush dipped in cold water, to ensure all sugar crystals are dissolved, as even one grain can cause the syrup to crystallize. Cook until sugar turns a dark golden color, about 5 to 8 minutes. When the caramel is ready, carefully pour in the warm cream and whisk until the sauce is smooth. Serve warm or at room temperature.

Stem Ginger with Shredded Duck

Yields 4 servings

Young pink stem ginger is usually available in the spring and early fall. Buy more than you can use and save it in some sherry in the refrigerator (see page 96). You will have the added bonus of ginger-flavored sherry to use in this dish or to add to desserts. This is the correct ginger to use for the common ginger beef dish you see on every Chinese restaurant menu. Use generously, as the flavor—though pungent—is not sharp.

    1 whole boneless, skinless duck breast, about 8 ounces
    1 teaspoon thin soy sauce
    2 teaspoons cornstarch
    1 tablespoon sherry
    1 tablespoon vegetable oil
    2 scallions, green and white parts minced
    1/2 cup stem ginger (*tsee geung*), cut into small cubes
    1 tablespoon yellow bean paste or light miso
    1 teaspoon sugar
    1/4 cup unsalted or low-sodium chicken stock or water

Cut the duck breast into thin shreds. In a small bowl, mix duck with soy sauce, cornstarch, and sherry. Set aside.

Heat the oil in a wok over medium heat, add the scallions, and stir-fry until aromatic, about 30 seconds. Add the duck and cook, tossing until it loses its pink color, then add the ginger, bean paste, sugar, and stock. Bring to a simmer and cook another minute or two, tossing to coat the duck with the sauce. Serve hot.

Water Chestnut
Ma Tai · Ma Ti
Eleocharis dulcis

Most of my favorite childhood snacks were not sweet. One was fresh water chestnuts, and anyone who has eaten fresh water chestnuts will understand this immediately. They are so different from the canned kind that they are almost two different vegetables.

Fresh water chestnuts—which are not nuts at all, but rather corms, or little bulbs—are the same size as true chestnuts, but they have a soft skin rather than a shell, and a flattened bottom with a tufted top. *Ma tai* translates as "horse's hooves," which the corm resembles. The skins are dark mahogany, with lighter brown triangular leaf scales around the top half. Unpeeled water chestnuts tend to be covered with dried dirt, as this corm grows in muddy water.

Canned water chestnuts are readily available and are used in many dishes. Although a poor substitute for the fresh, they come peeled and ready to use, which probably accounts for their popularity. Interestingly, the Cantonese rarely use water chestnuts as a vegetable, preferring their sweet crunchiness eaten out of hand as a snack. They will chop some up with minced meats and put them in dumpling fillings, and since they consider them "healthy," they also often add water chestnuts to tonic soups. You will sometimes find sautéed slices of a savory pudding made from water chestnuts as part of dim sum cuisine.

How to Use
Fresh water chestnuts turn soft and powdery as they deteriorate, so select firm ones. Peel the water chestnuts with a paring knife and hold in a bowl of cold water to prevent discoloration. Trim off any yellow or dark spots, and discard any soft or yellowed ones. The water chestnuts can be eaten raw, used in salads, served with fruit, minced and mixed with meat, and added to stir-fried dishes and soups.

Storage and Care
Store fresh water chestnuts in a brown paper bag in the vegetable bin of the refrigerator for up to several weeks. If peeled, they can be kept refrigerated in lightly salted cold water in a covered container for about one week.

Cultivation Tips
Not feasible for the home gardener.

Yields 4 to 6 servings

Preparing the fresh water chestnuts for this dish is a bit tedious, but the sweet crunch makes it well worthwhile. I intended this recipe to be formed in a heatproof bowl and steamed in the Chinese manner for a home-style savory meat cake, but baking it in the oven like a meat loaf is easier and as delicious.

Traditionally, the Chinese use ground pork, but the chicken makes a good low-fat dish and is not at all dry. It is interesting to note that Chinese cooks do not use an egg to bind this meat loaf.

> ½ pound fresh water chestnuts (*ma tai*)
> 1 pound ground chicken
> 2 tablespoons dry white wine
> 2 teaspoons thin soy sauce
> 1 teaspoon salt
> ¼ teaspoon freshly ground black pepper
> 1 tablespoon vegetable oil
> 1 teaspoon minced fresh ginger
> 1 tablespoon cornstarch
> ½ cup coarsely chopped cilantro leaves, lightly packed
> 1 teaspoon roasted sesame oil
>
> FOR THE SAUCE:
> ½ cup hoisin sauce
> 2 teaspoons dark soy sauce
> 2 tablespoons roasted sesame oil
>
> •
> Cilantro sprigs, for garnish

Preheat the oven to 350°F.

Peel the water chestnuts and hold in a bowl of cold water as you work. Coarsely chop by hand and set aside.

In a large bowl, combine the chicken, wine, thin soy sauce, salt, pepper, oil, ginger, and cornstarch. Toss with a large fork or hands to blend well, but do not overwork the mixture. Add the water chestnuts and cilantro, and toss to mix well.

Combine the ingredients for the sauce.

Grease a 9 x 5-inch loaf pan with additional sesame oil and lightly pack in the loaf mixture. Bake in the oven for 30 minutes. Brush with 2 to 4 tablespoons of the sauce and continue baking until the juices run clear when the meat loaf is pricked, another 10 to 15 minutes. Remove from the oven and let stand 10 minutes. Unmold or serve directly from loaf pan. Sprinkle with cilantro sprigs and serve remaining sauce on the side.

Horned Water Chestnut
Ling Kok · Ling Jiao
Trapa bicornis

During the Second World War, we lived as refugees in Macao. There were many privations, but lack of playmates was not one of them. There were many children, and lifelong friendships were formed. But a scarcity of store-bought toys was something we all noticed. We had to make up toys and games with what we had on hand. Of course, we needed jewelry for dress-ups, and as there was very little to use, we begged a *ling kok* or two from the kitchen. This shiny horned water chestnut, looking a little like a flying bat, made an interesting medallion when we poked holes in the horns and pushed string through it to form a necklace. We would sit for hours, shining our *ling kok* jewelry with bits of cloth. When we had had enough, we would shell them and return them to the kitchen. These nuts could not be eaten raw, because they contain toxins that have to be removed by cooking.

You cannot fail to recognize these nuts which have only recently become available in North American Asian markets. They are confusingly also called water chestnuts, but look entirely different with a hard, shiny black shell and two distinctive horns or wings. The nuts usually measure 2 inches from wing tip to wing tip, and are about 1 inch high in the center. When shelled the inner meat is ivory colored, starchy, and a little sweet. The chestnuts lose some of their crunchiness when cooked.

Horned water chestnut, or water caltrop, is a true water plant with diamond-shaped leaves and inflated stems that keep the plant floating. It is related to two other nuts, the Singhara nut (*trapa bispinosa*), common in Kashmir; and the four-horned Jesuits' nut (*trapa natans*), a common food for ancient Europeans. Horned water chestnut has been a food of China since ancient times. In everyday cooking today, however, the more common water chestnut (*ma tai*) is preferred.

How to Use
Horned water chestnuts must be shelled and cooked; they should never be eaten raw. A nutcracker will make an easier job of the shelling. The nuts can be steamed or boiled and served like potatoes; the Cantonese like them during the Moon Festival. They are also very good braised with meats or boiled in soup.

Storage and Care

Nuts can be kept several weeks in the refrigerator. They shrivel as they deteriorate, but this is difficult to ascertain through the hard shell. The meat should be ivory white, firm, and unblemished.

Cultivation Tips

Not feasible for the home gardener.

Horned Water Chestnuts

Yields 2 to 4 servings

Although this exotic-looking water chestnut is seldom seen in New York's Asian markets, they are more frequently available in California. If you find some, this is a good way to try them. Cracking the shells is tiresome and the water chestnuts *must* be cooked, but you should taste them at least once. They can, of course, be stir-fried and used in place of the more common water chestnuts after they have been parboiled.

> 1 pound horned water chestnuts (*ling kok*)
> 2 tablespoons butter
> 1 tablespoon minced fresh parsley or chives
> Salt and pepper

Using a nutcracker, shell the nuts. Place in a pot of cold water, bring to a boil, and simmer until tender, about 10 minutes. Drain. Toss in butter and herbs, season to taste with salt and pepper, and serve.

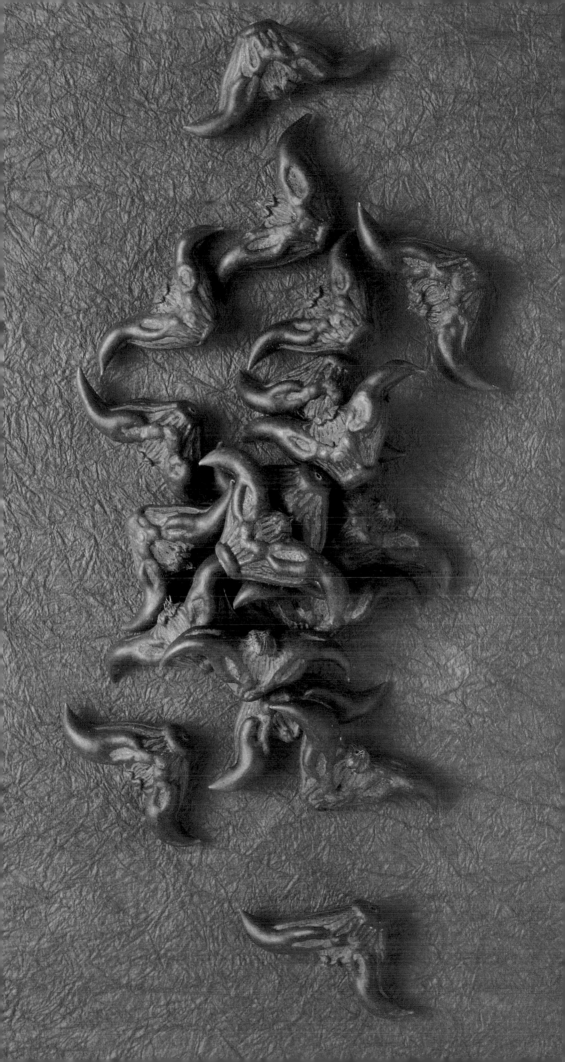

Green and White Daikon
Tseng Loh Bak, Loh Bak · Quing Luo Bo, Luo Bo
Raphanus sativus 'longipinnatus' or radicola

The Cantonese like to make a savory pudding with shredded daikon. This must be one of the most well-loved dishes using daikon because, whenever I meet a Chinese friend from Hong Kong and mention how I am now involved in food, I get offered a recipe for *loh bak go*, as we call this daikon (or turnip) pudding. To date I have at least three versions beautifully typed out and sent to me by friends, and notes of innumerable versions described to me in person. Much as we love this pudding, however, I rarely encounter the same enthusiasm from my students or American friends.

Making this pudding the old-fashioned way involves a number of steps. The daikon has to be shredded and soaked, the bits of meat that go into the pudding finely cut up, the mixture stirred over low heat, then the puddings formed and steamed. If you are fortunate enough to be around when the *loh bak go* is ready, it is spooned out and eaten hot. More often, however, large quantities are made, cooled, sliced, and then sautéed. A thin crisp skin forms on the outside, while the pudding warms and remains soft inside. The latter is the way you will find it in dim sum restaurants, and it is the way it is most often served for breakfast at home.

Daikon is used in many different ways. Additionally, there are many varieties with different shapes and sizes, including a rosy-hearted type grown in the cold climates of northern China that can be carved into the most beautiful roses for a garnish.

There are two kinds of daikon found here. The most common is the long, white daikon (*loh bak*), cylindrical in shape and usually measuring 3 to 4 inches across at its thickest and about 10 inches long, although they can be smaller or much larger. The flesh is white. The other type is the green daikon (*tseng loh bak*), which has a thin green skin that runs about two-thirds down the vegetable and green-tinged flesh. Green daikon must be cooked before eating. There are smaller types and even round types, but these are rarely available in markets.

Daikon can be sweet, sharp, and even spicy when eaten raw, with a radishlike flavor. It has a strong turniplike aroma and a tendency to discolor and give off water when left standing after being peeled. When cooked, daikon sweetens in flavor. It has a crisp texture, like a turnip, but is usually juicier.

Green Daikon

How to Use

Peeled daikon can be shredded—a common Japanese garnish—or pickled, braised, steamed, stir-fried, boiled or deep-fried.

Storage and Care

Buy crisp, hard, heavy daikon. They should be refrigerated and will last a week or longer. Wash and peel just before use.

Cultivation Tips

Daikon is a cool-weather vegetable and should be sown in late summer to autumn. As there are many varieties with different growing seasons, consult your seed catalog for those best suited to your area.

White Daikon Savory Pudding

Yields about 16 servings

This is the famous daikon pudding served as dim sum, sliced and sautéed until slightly crisp on the outside. When it is made at home, it is often served the first day, spooned out as a soft, savory pudding. The next day the cold pudding is sliced and fried as a popular breakfast food. I like it with a little soy sauce drizzled over and with a generous dab of hot sauce. If you want to avoid the frying, this pudding can be successfully reheated in a microwave.

> 3^1/$_4$ pounds white daikon (*loh bak*)
> 2 Chinese sausages
> 1 strip (about 3 ounces) Chinese bacon, or 2 ounces Smithfield ham
> ^{1}/$_4$ cup dried shrimp, soaked in warm water
> 8 to 10 dried black mushrooms, soaked in 1 cup of warm water
> 2 cups unsalted or low-sodium chicken stock
> ^{1}/$_2$ pound rice flour
> 1 tablespoon salt
> 1 teaspoon freshly ground black pepper
> 2 tablespoons white sesame seeds
> 2 scallions, green and white parts minced

Peel and grate the daikon by hand or in a food processor. There should be about 6 cups. Place in a large pot and cover with water. Bring to a boil, lower heat, and simmer until tender, about 15 minutes. Drain, reserving the cooking liquid.

Dice the sausages and bacon into small cubes. Drain the shrimp, discarding the water, and chop coarsely. Drain the mushrooms, reserving ^{1}/$_2$ cup of the soaking liquid, and chop coarsely. Combine the sausage, bacon, shrimp, and mushrooms in a bowl, mixing well. Set aside.

In a large bowl, combine the stock, 2 cups of the reserved daikon liquid, and the 1/2 cup mushroom water. Stir in the rice flour to make a thin batter. Season with salt and pepper. Fold in the grated daikon and reserved meats, shrimp, and mushrooms. Blend well and transfer to a large saucepan. Cook over medium heat, stirring constantly, until the mixture thickens, 5 to 7 minutes.

Oil two 8- or 9-inch cake pans. Divide the mixture evenly into the pans. Place in stacked bamboo steamer baskets and steam 1½ to 2 hours, until the puddings are set.

Scatter the sesame seeds and scallions over the tops of the puddings and steam another 5 minutes. Serve warm directly from pans, or cool completely and slice to fry.

Green Daikon and Sparerib Soup

Yields 4 to 6 servings

This hearty soup was suggested to me by my student Melody Santos. Unlike white daikon, which is quite pleasant raw in salads, green daikon has a very sharp taste and is best cooked to mellow the flavor. This soup could be a one-pot meal when spooned over white rice.

> 1½ pounds green daikon (*tseng loh bak*)
> 1½ pounds meaty pork spareribs
> 1 tablespoon vegetable oil
> 2 slices fresh ginger
> 1 medium onion, quartered
> 4 plum tomatoes, quartered
> 1 lemongrass stalk, coarse leaves removed and stalk sliced
> 1 tablespoon fish sauce (*nuoc mam* or *nam pla*)
> 1 ounce tamarind pulp, soaked in ½ cup hot water
> 2 tablespoons minced hot chili pepper
> Juice of 1 lime

Peel the daikon and cut into 2-inch cubes. Cut the spareribs into bite-size pieces using a cleaver or heavy chefs' knife (or ask your butcher to do it).

In a large pot or saucepan, heat the oil and sauté the ginger until brown. Remove and discard. Add the daikon, spareribs, onion, tomatoes, lemongrass, fish sauce, the water from the tamarind, the chili pepper, and 8 cups water. Bring the soup to the boil, reduce the heat, and simmer 1 to 1½ hours, or until soup is tasty and the meat is tender. Add the lime juice and serve.

Lotus Root
Leen Ngau · Lian Ou
Nelumbo nucifera

The beautiful lotus plant has a long and storied history in Asia. It has figured prominently in paintings of the ancient cultures of China and India where the Buddhist religion has dominated. In Buddhism, the lotus signifies peace and harmony, and the magnificent blossoms are a symbol of man's rebirth. Additionally, nearly every part of this plant has a role in food: seeds, flowers, stems, leaves, and roots. Lotus root has been a food in China since the Han Dynasty (207 B.C.–A.D. 220), and its valued role in Chinese culture is carried through to this day.

Although we are mainly concerned with the root, I should mention that the stems are also edible. The seeds are considered to be medicinally beneficial and are used in soups and stuffings or dried as a snack. The flowers are edible and can be scattered as a garnish over finished dishes for a beautiful effect. And the leaves are dried and used as wrappers for various dishes to which they impart a subtle perfume.

A favorite Cantonese tonic soup is prepared by boiling pork bones, a whole piece of belly pork, and lotus root. The vegetable is then sliced with the pork and served drizzled with soy sauce, while the soup is drunk for health. A small handful of barley may be added to the soup. This is another one of the "cooling" soups our amah prepared when she thought we needed to improve our general state of health.

Fresh lotus root is so exotic looking that if you see it you will be forced to find out what it is. It looks like a very large string of sausages, a series of bulbous shapes, each about 2 to 3 inches in diameter, and 4 or 5 inches long. The outer layer is the color of old ivory, with irregular dark brown streaks. When the root is sliced, the air passages that run through the bulb form a lacy pattern. Western chefs prize this quality, and use lotus root most often as a garnish. Although a woody, starchy vegetable, it has a mildly sweet flavor and a crisp texture that holds up well when cooked.

How to Use
Wash well and separate the sections, removing and discarding the "necks" in between. Peel. Lotus root can be cooked in large whole pieces, or stuffed, or sliced to reveal its unique pattern. It can be candied, pickled, boiled in soups, braised, or deep-fried.

Storage and Care

Buy a firm, unblemished root. Store in the refrigerator, but use within three to five days of purchase. Wash well and peel just before using.

Cultivation Tips

As with most of the other water plants, lotus is not easily grown in a home garden. People with backyard ponds use it as an ornamental plant, but if you eat it, you destroy the garden effect.

Candied Lotus Root

Yields approximately 1 cup

Because lotus root slices have a pretty lacy pattern, I thought of candying them to use as a garnish or topping for dessert. They keep their shape well, and have a chestnutlike texture that works well with creamy mousse desserts, ice cream, and even something crunchy, like a fruit-filled tuille.

> 1/2 pound lotus root (*leen ngau*), peeled and sliced 1/4 inch thick

> FOR THE SYRUP:
> 1 cup sugar
> 2 slices fresh ginger
> 1 star anise
> 1 piece lemon peel, 1/2 inch by 2 inches
> 1 tablespoon lemon juice

Place the lotus slices in a saucepan and cover with water. Bring to a boil and cook 5 minutes. Drain and repeat twice more.

In a heavy saucepan, bring the sugar, 1 cup water, ginger, star anise, lemon peel, and lemon juice to a boil. Add the lotus root, return to a boil, reduce the heat and simmer 40 minutes to 1 hour, or until syrup is thick and lotus slices are tender. The lotus root will darken slightly and have a texture like chestnuts.

Note: If you keep it covered in its syrup in the refrigerator, it will keep for months. If syrup gets too thick, dilute with a little water.

See photograph on pages 94–95.

Taro
Woo Tau, Woo Chai · Yu Tou, Yu Zi
Colocasia esculenta

Taro dumplings, little turnovers of mashed taro, are filled with bits of chopped meat, mushrooms, and bamboo shoots. When the turnover is deep-fried, the taro develops a crispy lacy layer with a soft interior. Mashed taro, when used in dumplings, is very much like mashed potatoes and, when used in dumplings, combines the two ways people most like potatoes—crunchy fries and comforting mashed potatoes.

There are more than 200 varieties of taro, which has been a staple food for 2,000 years, not only in Asia but also in Africa and Polynesia. Today, two types are grown for Asian markets. They are drastically different in size, but taste the same and can be used in the same way. The large betel nut taro (*woo tau*), usually 4 inches across and 6 to 8 inches long, has a hairy brown skin and pale mauve flesh lightly veined in red. The small red-budded taro (*woo chai*) are the duck egg-size baby tubers that surround a central root. These also are covered in a hairy brown skin, and the Cantonese like to boil them in their jackets, then peel and eat them, sprinkled with sugar. They are starchy like a potato, with a bland, slightly sweet taste.

How to Use
Large taro should be peeled and cut up before cooking. Small taro can be boiled or baked in their jackets. Both varieties are good mashed, braised, steamed, and fried.

Storage and Care
Store dry in the refrigerator or at room temperature for a few days.

Cultivation Tips
Not feasible for home gardeners.

Taro Turnovers

Yields 30 turnovers

FOR THE DOUGH:
1 pound peeled taro (*woo tau*)
4 tablespoons lard or vegetable shortening
3 tablespoons cornstarch
2 teaspoons sugar
1 teaspoon salt

FOR THE FILLING:

4 ounces lean pork loin

1 tablespoon plus 1 teaspoon thin soy sauce

1 teaspoon cornstarch

2 ounces shrimp, shelled and deveined

4 dried black mushrooms, soaked in warm water for 20 minutes

1 teaspoon sugar

1 teaspoon roasted sesame oil

2 teaspoons vegetable oil

1 tablespoon cornstarch, mixed with 4 tablespoons cold water

Salt and pepper

•

1 cup cornstarch, for dusting turnovers

4 cups vegetable oil, for deep-frying

Make the dough. Cut the peeled taro into chunks and place in a bamboo steamer. Steam over boiling water until soft, 30 to 40 minutes. Remove to a bowl and mash thoroughly with a potato masher or put through a ricer. Mix the warm mashed taro with the lard, cornstarch, sugar, and salt. Mix well, cover, and cool completely. The dough may be made ahead, wrapped well, and refrigerated several days.

Make the filling. Cut the pork into very small slivers. Mound together and chop a few times. Combine the pork with 1 teaspoon soy sauce and the 1 teaspoon cornstarch. Let stand 5 to 10 minutes. Meanwhile, chop the shrimp into small bits. Drain the mushrooms and chop into small pieces. In a small bowl, combine the remaining 1 tablespoon soy sauce, sugar, and sesame oil.

In a wok, heat the 2 teaspoons oil. Stir-fry the pork, shrimp, and mushrooms until the pork and shrimp are cooked, about 2 minutes. Add the soy sauce mixture and stir to blend. Add the cornstarch mixture, bringing to a boil until sauce thickens and binds the ingredients together. Remove to a bowl, season with salt and pepper to taste, cover, and chill until cold.

To form the turnovers, divide the dough into 3 parts. Roll each into a thick sausage and cut into 10 equal pieces. Between your palms, roll each piece into a ball, then flatten into a circle, $2\frac{1}{2}$ to 3 inches in diameter. Place a scant teaspoonful of filling in the center of each circle, fold over, and pinch edges together to seal. Repeat until all the turnovers are formed. Roll them in cornstarch to coat well.

Heat the 4 cups oil in a wok to 425°F. Deep-fry the turnovers a few at a time until golden and crunchy bits form on the outside. Do not overbrown. Drain on paper towels and serve warm or at room temperature.

Small Taro

Sweet Potato
Fan Sue · Fan Shu, Gan Shu
Ipomoea batatas

In Hong Kong, in the years immediately after the Second World War, it was not uncommon for young girls to lack knowledge of cooking. In the houses of most of my relatives and friends, the kitchens were run by the cooks, and children were never encouraged to mess about in them. The hours between lunch and dinner, however, were usually quiet ones in the kitchen. We would often sneak in to prepare something special for our afternoon tea. Our friend Gladys was an "expert," and one of her favorite after-school snacks was a sweet soup with cubes of sweet potato floating in it. Sweet potato was a common staple, and we could always find one or two.

Sweet potatoes need no introduction for most of us. We are all familiar with the sweet potato casseroles and pies served at Thanksgiving. But sweet potatoes are very popular with the Chinese, too, and you will find them in Asian markets practically year-round. Although there are many varieties of sweet potatoes, those most common have a reddish skin and a deep yellow interior. Some have paler skins and redder or even purple centers. They are all highly nutritious, rich in beta-carotene. Oval and bumpier, sweet potatoes are less mealy than white potatoes.

How to Use
Sweet potatoes are used in sweet and savory soups, are mashed for fillings in dumplings, and are deep-fried. They are also very good baked.

Storage and Care
Look for firm, unblemished potatoes for a longer shelf life. Store in a cool room or refrigerator. Wash and peel before cutting into desired shape and size for use, or use unpeeled.

Cultivation Tips
Sweet potatoes are easy to grow from slips in warm, sunny climates. They stop growing if the temperature falls to 60°F. Plant slips in poor, dry, slightly acid, and well-drained soil. Many growers mound the plants to improve drainage.

Yields 10 servings

This sweet potato pudding is light, and the bits of fresh and crystallized ginger add interesting elements to the texture as well as the flavor. You can serve it warm or cold, with whipped cream or Ginger Caramel Sauce (page 98). It makes a nice dessert for the winter holidays. Although a copper bowl is best for whipping the egg whites, if you do not have one, use a clean metal or glass bowl and add $1/4$ teaspoon cream of tartar to help them mount well.

> $1/4$ cup plus 2 tablespoons granulated sugar
> 2 pounds sweet potato (*fan sue*)
> 6 slices fresh ginger
> $1/2$ cup heavy cream
> $1/2$ cup crystallized ginger (about 2 ounces)
> 4 egg yolks
> 2 tablespoons flour
> 6 egg whites
> Pinch of salt
> Confectioners' sugar, for dusting

Preheat the oven to 350°F. Generously butter a 9- or 10-inch casserole dish about 4 inches high, then dust with 2 tablespoons granulated sugar, shaking well to evenly coat the dish.

Peel the sweet potatoes and cut into chunks. Cook in 6 cups cold water with the 6 slices ginger until tender, about 20 minutes. Drain and reserve the potatoes and ginger. Mash the potatoes with a large fork or potato masher. Stir in the cream to lighten the potatoes. Mince the reserved ginger, and coarsely chop the crystallized ginger. Fold into the mashed potatoes.

With a mixer, beat the egg yolks and remaining $1/4$ cup sugar until light and lemon colored. Stir in the flour and beat until smooth. With a large rubber spatula, fold the mashed potatoes into the egg mixture.

In a clean copper bowl, whip the egg whites with a pinch of salt until stiff but not dry. Fold one-third of the egg whites into the potato mixture to lighten it, then fold the rest of the egg whites into the mixture. Do not overfold.

Pour into the prepared casserole dish and bake until a skewer pricked into the center comes out clean, about 1 hour and 15 minutes. The pudding will rise up and fall as it cools. Remove from the oven, dust with confectioners' sugar, and serve warm or cold.

Jicama
Sa Kot · Sha Ge
Pachyrhizus erosus

The common name for this tuber is an example of why this book is needed. I was introduced to jicama thinking it was a Mexican vegetable, but once I tried it, I realized that it was what the Chinese call *sa kot*, or yam bean. Up until then, I thought of *sa kot* as a Chinese vegetable and had usually eaten it cooked, most often stir-fried with beef. I loved the crunch, which was much like water chestnuts, but preferred its sweeter taste to that of bland canned water chestnuts.

Jicama is a native plant of the Americas, grown for its edible tubers. It was embraced by southern Asians after it was introduced to the Philippines in the seventeenth century. It is called yam bean, because this vegetable grows on an annual vine that produces pods and fruit. The mature pods contain rotenone, which is poisonous and should not be eaten, but the tuber is fresh tasting and sweet. It makes a good substitute for water chestnuts and bamboo shoots in Asian cooking. Unfortunately, it is not highly nutritious, so jicama is eaten mostly for pleasure.

Jicama ranges in size from 4 inches in diameter to 6 or 8 inches. It has a narrow neck and a lobed bottom. The dark beige outer skin is easily peeled to reveal white flesh that is juicy and crunchy. Jicama are available in many supermarkets as well as Asian markets. However, when buying them in winter, be sure they have not frozen, as the flesh turns translucent and mushy.

How to Use
Peel both the dark outer skin and the fibrous white inner layer. Cut into desired shapes. Jicama can be creamed, steamed, braised, used in soups, stir-fried, and deep-fried. Because of its bland flavor, it marries well with almost anything.

Storage and Care
Select firm, heavy fruit free of blemishes. Store at room temperature for several days or refrigerate for longer storage. Do not freeze.

Cultivation Tips
This annual vine is a tropical plant and requires hot temperatures and a long growing season, therefore I do not recommend it for the home gardener.

Yields 1 quart

The Chinese like jicama for its crunchy texture in stir-fried dishes. This recipe uses it raw—the jicama can be served simply as a spicy pickle or as crudité with a minty yogurt dip, or the sticks can be wrapped with prosciutto and served as an appetizer.

> 1 jicama, about 1 pound (*sa kot*)
> 2 tablespoons rice vinegar
> $^1/_2$ teaspoon black mustard seeds
> 1 teaspoon sugar
> $^1/_4$ teaspoon salt
> $^1/_4$ teaspoon cayenne (or less if you prefer)
> 1 teaspoon lemon juice

Peel the jicama, cut it into slices about $^1/_2$ inch thick, and then cut slices into sticks.

In a bowl, toss together the vinegar, mustard seeds, sugar, salt, cayenne, and lemon juice. Mix well. Add the jicama and toss to coat well. Cover and refrigerate overnight before serving.

Kohlrabi
Gai Lan Tau · Jie Lan Tou
Brassica oleracea, Gongylodes group

Kohlrabi, which is the same species as Chinese broccoli but a different subspecies, is a modern introduction to Asia. You cannot mistake this round vegetable with cut-off stalk ends growing from the top and sides. The pale green balls measure 2 to 4 inches in diameter, and sometimes have a few leaves attached as well. The flesh is creamy white, firm, with a slight cabbage flavor and applelike texture.

How to Use
Kohlrabi can be eaten raw or cooked. For Asian dishes, stems, leaves, and base should be cut off and discarded, and the root peeled. Cut as desired for braising, steaming, or stir-frying with meat or poultry. Or the whole unpeeled knob can be parboiled, then peeled and cut into chunks, added to salads, or cooked further.

Storage and Care
Choose unblemished small kohlrabi, as larger ones can be tough and woody. They should keep a week or longer in the refrigerator.

Cultivation Tips
Kohlrabi is quite easily grown. Home gardeners can also grow a purple variety, which is not available in Asian markets.

Kohlrabi Tossed in Butter

Yields 4 servings

This vegetable, popular with the Chinese, has a delicate mustardy flavor that is enhanced when served simply. Be sure to pick the smallest ones, and peel them deeply to remove tough woody outer parts.

> 4 small kohlrabi (*gai lan tau*), about 1 pound
> 1 tablespoon unsalted butter
> 2 tablespoons coarsely chopped fresh parsley
> $1/2$ teaspoon salt
> $1/4$ teaspoon freshly ground black pepper

Peel the kohlrabi heads. Cut into cubes, cover with cold water, and cook until tender, 15 to 20 minutes. Drain well.

Immediately toss with butter until well coated, then toss in parsley, salt, and pepper. Mix well and serve.

Kudzu
Fun Kot · Fen Ge
Pueraria thunbergiana (lobata)

Kudzu, an Asian native, has the same bulbous quality as jicama, but it is much larger and more ovate in shape, measuring 15 inches and even longer. It has a tan outer skin and a white flesh that is sweetish, but much more starchy than jicama. The flesh tends to be tough.

How to Use
Kudzu is used almost exclusively in soups because it produces a sweet-tasting broth; it is best cut into manageable pieces before peeling deeply and cutting into chunks, which are discarded after cooking.

Storage and Care
Store kudzu, like potatoes, at cool room temperature.

Cultivation Tips
Not recommended for home gardeners because it is invasive.

Kudzu Noodle Soup

Yields 2 to 4 servings

Once you've made the broth, this is a quick one-dish meal.

- ³⁄₄ to 1 pound kudzu (*fun kot*)
- 2 pounds beef bones
- 1 pound pork bones with meat
- 3 scallions, 2 whole and 1 minced
- 3 slices fresh ginger
- 1 cup cooked noodles or very thin spaghetti
- 1 cup sliced cooked meat, such as poached chicken, roast pork, or Chinese roast duck

In a large stockpot, combine the kudzu, beef and pork bones, 2 whole scallions, ginger, and 10 cups cold water. Bring to a boil, reduce the heat, skim off any foam, and simmer 3 to 4 hours. Strain the broth and discard the bones and vegetables.

Return the broth to a saucepan, add the cooked noodles, and simmer until noodles are hot, about 3 minutes. Divide into bowls, place cooked meat on top of noodles, and sprinkle with minced scallions before serving.

Chinese Arrowhead
Tse Goo · Ci Gu
Sagittaria sinensis

Arrowhead tubers are common in Asian markets during winter and spring. They are the size of water chestnuts and shaped like small eggs. A small shoot may sprout from the tip. The ivory-colored tubers are covered with a thin, brown, peeling skin. Arrowhead tubers have a sweet, slightly bitter, starchy taste, with some crunch.

How to Use
Peel arrowhead tubers and remove any sprouts. They can be cooked whole, sliced, or coarsely chopped. They can be braised, stir-fried with meat, steamed, mashed, or boiled and served like new potatoes.

Storage and Care
Buy firm tubers and store in a brown paper bag in the refrigerator for up to a week. Peel and rinse briefly before cutting into desired size.

Cultivation Tips
Arrowhead tubers are not feasible for the home gardener.

Arrowhead Tubers with Pork

Yields 2 servings

> 6–8 arrowhead tubers
> 8 ounces boneless pork loin
> 1 tablespoon vegetable oil
> 1 garlic clove, minced
> 1 teaspoon minced fresh ginger
> 1 scallion, green and white parts minced
> 1 tablespoon yellow bean sauce
> $1/3$ cup unsalted or low-sodium chicken stock or water
> $1/2$ teaspoon crushed Japanese pepper (sansho) or 1 teaspoon
>   freshly ground black pepper

Peel and slice the tubers. Cut the pork into thin slivers, about $1/4$ inch by 1 inch.

   In a wok, heat the oil and stir-fry the garlic, ginger, and scallions until aromatic, about 30 seconds. Add the pork, yellow bean paste, and tubers. Stir-fry 1 minute, tossing often. Add stock and pepper. Bring to a boil, reduce the heat, and simmer 3 to 5 minutes, until the tubers are tender. Serve hot.

Sprouts·
Shoots
& Beans

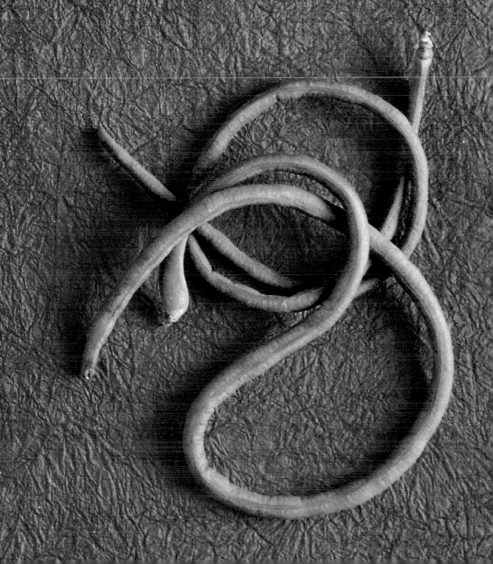

Soybean Sprouts
Daai Dau Nga Choy · Da Dou Ya Cai
Glycine max

大豆芽菜

Soybeans have been cultivated in China for more than 4,000 years.
Highly nutritious soybeans and all the products made from them, from
soy sauce to the different bean curd products, have provided protein
for China and many other Asian countries. It is no wonder, then, that
the Chinese would cultivate soybean sprouts as a vegetable. I am
particularly fond of stir-fried soybean sprouts plain or prepared with
beef or pork. I like the crunchy, nutty taste of the yellow bean tops
attached to the crunchy stem.

Last summer, while shopping in Chinatown, I saw soybean
sprouts for the first time. Although the sprouts are usually sold neatly
tied in bundles in Hong Kong, they are sold here in loose mounds, just
like mung bean sprouts. You will not confuse them, however, as these
sprouts have larger, bright yellow heads that measure about $1/4$ inch
long. The whole sprout is also larger, 2 to 3 inches long. The stems,
with roots attached, should be crisp and white, just like a mung bean
sprout.

How to Use
Buy sprouts with yellow heads that have no hint of green or blemishes.
The green-tinged ones, while not harmful, are not as tasty. The roots
should be trimmed off, if you have the patience and time. Unlike
mung bean sprouts, these should *never* be eaten raw. For use in
salads, blanch briefly in boiling water, then refresh in ice water and
drain. Soybean sprouts are usually used in soups, are stir-fried, and
sometimes, are coarsely chopped and mixed with ground meat to
provide crunch and texture.

Storage and Care
The sprouts are best used within a few days of purchase. Store in an
open plastic bag in the vegetable bin of the refrigerator for one or two
days. For longer storage, keep under cold water in a covered container
in the refrigerator. Cut off roots if desired, then rinse briefly in cold
water, drain, and use as desired.

Cultivation Tips
Not recommended.

Yields 4 servings

In Chinatown, you will see mounds of these sprouts alongside the more common mung bean sprouts. The larger yellow heads are crunchier and stand up well to stir-frying. You can substitute beef flank strips for the pork, if you prefer. This is a really quick stir-fry that is simple and good for everyday meals.

1 pound soybean sprouts (*daai dau nga choy*)
1/2 pound pork tenderloin

FOR THE MARINADE:
2 teaspoons thin soy sauce
2 teaspoons cornstarch

•

2 tablespoons fermented black beans
2 garlic cloves, mashed
1 tablespoon vegetable oil

FOR THE SAUCE:
2 teaspoons thin soy sauce
1/3 cup unsalted or low-sodium chicken stock or water
2 teaspoons cornstarch

Wash and spin-dry the sprouts in a salad spinner. Set aside.

Cut the pork into thin strips and mix with the soy sauce and cornstarch for the marinade. Let stand 10 minutes.

Rinse the black beans to remove excess salt. In a small bowl, lightly mash the beans with the garlic. Add the oil and mix well.

Combine the sauce ingredients in a bowl.

Heat a wok. Add the black bean mixture and stir-fry 10 seconds. Add the pork and stir-fry, tossing frequently, until the pork loses its pink color, 3 to 5 minutes. Add the sprouts, toss once or twice, then add the sauce ingredients, making sure that the cornstarch is mixed in well. Continue to toss and stir-fry until the sauce thickens, about 1 minute. Serve immediately.

Mung Bean Sprouts
Nga Choy · Ya Cai
Phaseolus aureus (Vigna radiata)

When I left Hong Kong for London, it was the first time I lived away from home. Naturally, I was homesick and one of the things I longed for was familiar food. The only mung bean sprouts to be had were discolored limp threads in cans. Even after soaking in ice water, the sprouts were hopelessly mushy. Since then, I have learned how to grow juicy, crisp, fat mung bean sprouts at home. But since top-grade commercially grown sprouts are now available, it's no trouble to enjoy fresh bean sprouts anytime.

Mung bean sprouts have been cultivated in China for more than 5,000 years as an economical, highly nutritious vegetable. To supply enough bean sprouts for the millions of people who love them, growers have developed sophisticated methods of production. The beans sprout best in a warm moist medium, but as they are highly perishable, the tops of the tiny sprouts must be kept cool, so they are usually washed with cold water several times a day. To get fat, juicy sprouts, they are also weighted. Mung bean sprouts are sold piled high, in large plastic bags. The pale yellow seeds have usually lost their green coats, although some may be still attached. Delicate white stems measuring 2 to 4 inches long usually have the root ends still attached. The sprouts have a very delicate flavor, and so are valued for their crisp texture and nutritional content.

How to Use
Rinse briefly in cold water and drain well. When cleaning a large quantity, I like to spin the sprouts briefly in a salad spinner. They are generally used as is, but you can nip off the tops and bottoms for "silver sprouts." They can be eaten raw or blanched briefly and used in soups, stuffings (as in egg rolls), or quickly stir-fried.

Storage and Care
Bean sprouts are highly perishable and are best used within a day or two. If they are very fresh, however, they can be kept up to a week in a sealed plastic container in the refrigerator. Do not let them get overwet, as they will disintegrate rapidly. Some people like to keep sprouts in cold water, but I find they become waterlogged.

Cultivation Tips

Commercial cultivation yields a better quality bean sprout. I do not recommend sprouting your own except as an interesting project. If you must sprout your own, best results are achieved in a sprouter, which can be acquired at a good health food store, and following the directions. Be sure to use beans meant expressly for sprouting.

Mung Bean Sprout Salad

Yields 4 to 6 servings

Second to snow peas, this is probably the best known Chinese vegetable. These sprouts are very perishable, but if you buy them crisp and fresh from an Asian market, this is a great refreshing way to serve them.

1 pound mung bean sprouts (*nga choy*)

FOR THE DRESSING:
2 tablespoons minced shallots
2 garlic cloves, minced
1 teaspoon minced fresh ginger
$\frac{1}{2}$ cup unsalted or low-sodium chicken stock
1 tablespoon dry sherry
2 tablespoon olive oil
1 teaspoon salt
$\frac{1}{2}$ teaspoon freshly ground black pepper
1 tablespoon minced fresh spearmint or peppermint
2 scallions, green and white parts minced

Rinse the bean sprouts and spin-dry in a salad spinner. Place in a serving bowl.

Make the dressing. In a small bowl, whisk together the shallots, garlic, ginger, stock, sherry, olive oil, salt, and pepper until well blended. Stir in the mint.

Pour the dressing over the sprouts, sprinkle with scallions, and toss to blend well before serving.

Pea Shoots
Dau Mui · Dou Miao
Pisum sativum var. *macrocarpon*

Years ago I saw pea shoots in Chinatown only on rare occasions. Their scarcity and relatively light weight made them a high priced luxury. Today, thanks to their popularity with restaurant chefs, pea shoots are readily available, not only in Asian markets but also at specialty food stores and farmers' markets. In the spring and early summer, you see mounds of light green pea shoots piled high in the vegetable stalls of Chinatown. Of course, they still command a high price but no one seems to mind paying for them. I wonder if this is because their pretty tendrils proclaim their fragility.

Pea shoots are the tender leaves and tendrils of the snow pea plant. The tips are harvested when the plants are very young and the plants never mature. The leaves are oval, about 1 inch long by ½ inch wide, and light green. Ideally the shoots should be just the tips and tendrils with only the top pair of small leaves attached to the young stem. However, sometimes, the shoots include a few larger leaves; occasionally, there may be small white blossoms or buds. Although shoots may be grown from any variety of garden pea, snow pea shoots taste very subtly of snow peas.

How to Use
Obviously, this is a luxury vegetable, served for special occasions. The shoots can be eaten raw, possibly with a little lemon juice squeezed over them. They are used in soups, often with an expensive ingredient such as crabmeat; steamed, or stir-fried with meat, seafood, poultry; or wilted by themselves, usually with a little ginger and sugar. The shoots are good just wilted with olive oil and garlic.

Storage and Care
Pea shoots are very perishable. Buy only crisp, fresh shoots. Pea shoots should be stored wrapped in paper towels in an open plastic bag in the vegetable bin of the refrigerator. Use immediately, or within one or two days of purchase. Remove any coarse stems. Rinse quickly under cold water, then drain and spin-dry in a salad spinner.

Cultivation Tips
As with all peas, the snow peas planted for harvesting shoots require fertile, moisture-retentive, neutral soil. They are a cool-weather plant

and ideally should be grown when temperatures are between 55 and 65°F. Seeds can be sown closely where they are to grow and vines should be allowed to creep. Shoots should be picked when plants are 2 to 4 inches high. Pick off all flower buds to encourage vegetative growth. As with other peas, pea shoots have a very short season.

Pea Shoots with Velvet Shrimp

Yields 4 servings

In the past, pea shoots were used mostly when the tender shoots could be picked from the garden or farm. I have adapted a classic velvet shrimp recipe to include pea shoots; it is more common to find the dish made with snow peas.

> 3 to 4 cups lightly packed pea shoots (*dau mui*), about ¾ to 1 pound
> 1 pound medium shrimp, shelled and deveined
>
> FOR THE MARINADE:
> 1 egg white
> 2 teaspoons cornstarch
> 1 teaspoon vegetable oil
>
> •
>
> 2 tablespoons vegetable oil
> 1 scallion, green and white parts minced
> 1 teaspoon minced fresh ginger
> 2 garlic cloves, minced
> 2 tablespoons yellow bean sauce
> 2 teaspoons thin soy sauce
> ¼ cup water or unsalted or low-sodium chicken stock
> 2 teaspoons roasted sesame oil

Remove the tough stems from pea shoots and discard. Wash in cold water and spin-dry in a salad spinner. Set aside.

In a bowl, combine the shrimp with the egg white, cornstarch, and oil for the marinade. Let stand 20 minutes.

In a wok, heat the 2 tablespoons oil until just smoking. Add the scallion, ginger, and garlic and cook until aromatic, about 30 seconds. Add the shrimp and stir-fry, tossing constantly, until the shrimp just turn pink, 5 to 7 minutes. Add the yellow bean sauce, soy sauce, water, and pea shoots. Toss to wilt shoots, about 2 minutes.

Remove from the heat, drizzle with sesame oil, and stir to blend. Serve immediately.

Long Beans
Bak Dau Gok, Tseng Dau Gak · Dou Jiao
Vigna unguiculata ssp. *sesquipedalis*

豆
角

As a special project, I gave a Chinese cooking lesson to the students in my daughter's class when she was about twelve years old. As is invariably the case, there were two kids who were high-spirited and not really interested in cooking. I had planned to serve long beans as our vegetable, intending to cut them up and stir-fry them. However, as the class progressed I had to keep our rowdy two occupied, so I quickly blanched the long beans whole, cooled them, and set the boys to braiding them. They were immediately engrossed, and the class proceeded without further commotion. When we sat down to our meal we each had a beautiful braid of green beans garnishing the plate.

Long beans, also called yard-long beans, or asparagus beans, are easily distinguishable by their length, which can be up to 3 feet. This bean is a close relative of the cowpea (black-eyed pea) rather than the green bean. There are two varieties, a pale green one called *bak dau gok*, and a dark green type called *tseng dau gok*. The dark green bean is generally considered more delectable. Crunchier than green beans and with a slightly tougher texture, long beans can take a little more cooking without getting mushy. Although the flavor is similar, they do not taste exactly like green beans and are not a substitute. Even though they work well in green bean dishes, long beans bring their own characteristic flavor to a dish. Thinner beans with underdeveloped seeds are the best.

How to Use
Long beans are great simply blanched and tossed in sesame oil, served hot or at room temperature. They can also be deep-fried, stir-fried, cooked with meats and flavorful sauces, served hot or cold. The beans are usually cut into 1- to 2-inch lengths, but require no stringing.

Storage and Care
If the beans have not been sitting around too long, they will keep, loosely wrapped, in the refrigerator for up to ten days; I prefer to use the beans within a day or two of purchase. Do not let the beans become moist, as they will deteriorate rapidly. The beans come tied in a bunch, and I wash them still tied to facilitate cutting them. Discard the stem ends.

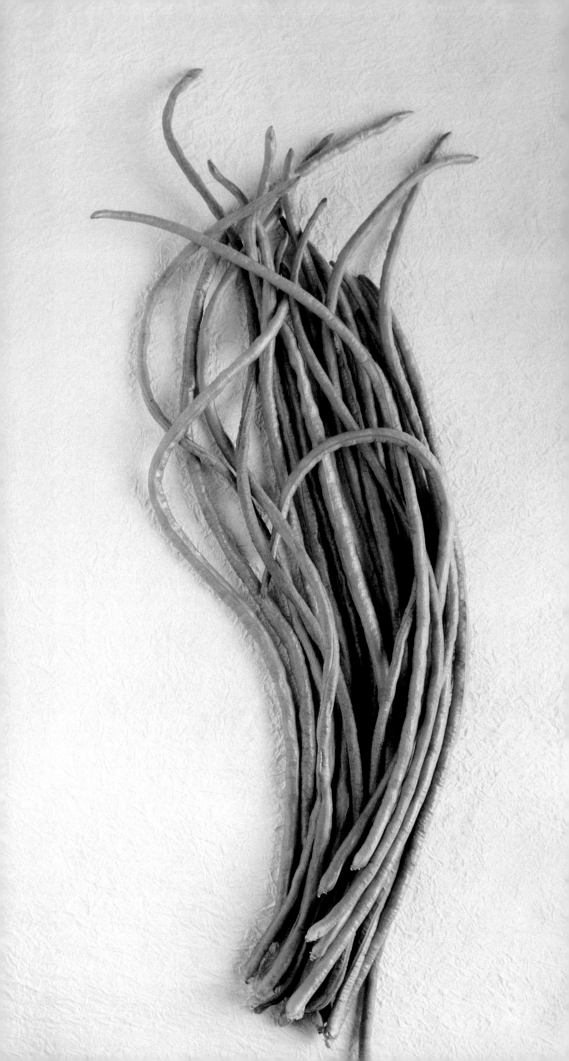

Cultivation Tips

Although this annual pole bean requires warm summers, it is fast growing and beans can be harvested in less than three months, when about 1 foot long. They like fertile acid soil, but are hardy and will grow in poorer soil with low rainfall. The beans need to be supported with a trellis or pole. Although never available in markets, the leaves and young stems are also edible, a plus for the home gardener.

Long Beans Dry-Fried with Peanuts and Spicy Sauce

Yields 2 to 4 servings

Long beans are perfect for this dish, because even with the double cooking, they do not become mushy. If you cannot find raw shelled peanuts, dry-roasted ones are a good substitute.

> $1/2$ pound long beans (*dau gok*)
> 2 cups vegetable oil
> $1/2$ cup raw shelled peanuts
> 1 teaspoon minced fresh ginger
> 1 garlic clove, minced
> 1 scallion, green and white parts minced
> 1 teaspoon chili paste (or more, if you really like it hot)
> $1/2$ cup unsalted or low-sodium chicken stock
> 1 tablespoon cornstarch, mixed with 2 tablespoons cold water

Leaving the long beans tied together for easy handling, wash them well in cold water. Cut into 2-inch pieces, discarding the ends. Dry well on paper towels.

In a wok, heat the oil to 400°F. Quickly pass the raw peanuts through the oil, until just golden, about 30 seconds to 1 minute. Remove and drain on paper towels.

Carefully add the long beans to the hot oil and deep-fry until they blister, about 5 minutes. Remove with a slotted spoon and drain on paper towels.

Pour off the oil and discard, but leave about 1 teaspoon in the wok. Return the wok to the heat. Add the ginger, garlic, and scallion and stir-fry until aromatic, about 30 seconds. Add the chili paste and stock, stir to blend, then add the cornstarch mixture. Bring to a boil and cook 1 minute or until sauce thickens. Return the beans to the wok and toss until coated and hot. Add the peanuts and quickly toss to mix well and serve.

See photograph on pages 128–129.

荷蘭豆

Snow Peas
Hoh Laan Dau · He Lan Dou
Pisum sativum var. *macrocarpum*

Even more than bean sprouts, snow peas are considered an Asian vegetable in the West, and they have certainly been on the scene for a long time. Indeed, it is the only Asian vegetable available frozen in practically every supermarket in the country. And yet its Chinese name translates as "Holland bean," signifying that to the Chinese this is a vegetable from the West. Snow peas have been eaten in China since the Tang Dynasty, seventh century A.D., so whatever its origins and however it is perceived, it is certainly one of the most "Asian" vegetables around.

Snow peas grow like English peas in a pod, but instead snow peas are eaten for the pods. In fact, the peas do not mature and the pods remain flat, tender, and sweet. They are a jade green, and often need a little stringing. For a special effect I cut a wedge shape in both ends of the pods. This is tedious and time-consuming, but the effort is a compliment to family and friends—an expression of love. After all, eating a wonderful meal together is a sensual joy that can be achieved simply.

How to Use
Buy crisp, unblemished snow peas. They can be parboiled and refreshed, eaten raw if very young and tender, steamed, stir-fried, sautéed, or simply tossed in butter or cooked with meat, poultry, or seafood. A favorite dish is snow peas with velvet chicken, where the bright jade vegetable contrasts with the white pieces of chicken for a perfect yin-yang effect.

Storage and Care
Keep refrigerated in the vegetable bin, loosely bagged. If peas are very fresh, they will keep well, up to two weeks. String, if necessary, trim as desired, and use whole or finely cut into strips.

Cultivation Tips
Grow this cool-weather vegetable for a spring or early summer crop, as you would English peas. Use a trellis and harvest in about 60 days. In hot climates, a second crop can be sown in the autumn for an early winter crop.

荷蘭豆

Yields 6 servings

Snow peas are so common that I use them here in a slightly different way. Select tender young pods for this lovely soup. I serve this with a small bit of infused ginger-thyme cream drizzled over the soup at the last minute.

FOR THE GINGER-THYME CREAM:
1 pint heavy cream
6 slices fresh ginger, cut into matchsticks
6 lemon thyme sprigs, or thyme sprigs

•

2 pounds tender young snow peas (*hoh laan dau*)
4 tablespoons unsalted butter
1 medium onion, minced
4 cups unsalted or low-sodium chicken stock
Salt and pepper
Thyme sprigs, for garnish (optional)

Make the ginger-thyme cream. In a small saucepan, combine the cream, ginger, and thyme sprigs. Bring to a simmer and cook over low heat for 20 minutes. Turn off heat and let stand 10 minutes. Strain and reserve.

While cream is cooking, string the snow peas, if necessary, and pinch off the ends. Wash and drain.

In a deep saucepan, over medium heat, melt the butter and sauté the onion until soft, stirring often so as not to burn it. Add the snow peas and stock, bring to a boil, reduce the heat, and simmer until the peas are tender, 10 to 15 minutes.

Strain the peas, reserving the stock. In a food processor or blender, puree the snow peas. Return the puree and reserved stock to the pan, season to taste with salt and pepper, and heat. Drizzle a bit of the ginger-thyme cream on each serving.

Bamboo Shoots
Chuk Sun · Zhu Sun

Dendrocalamus asper

竹筍

The bamboo plant—actually more than 60 species—has been painted by artists, celebrated in poetry and song, cultivated as much for its beauty as its usefulness. Bamboo wood is used to make furniture, luggage, storage containers, and articles for ceremonial uses. The leaves are used for clothing, food wrappers, and many utensils, some of which have culinary uses. And the shoots are eaten as a vegetable. During the Han Dynasty, bamboo slips were used to record "recipes" and food notes—to write an ancient cookbook, if you will.

Although not always available, fresh bamboo shoots are sold in Chinatown occasionally. You will often see large tubs of whole ivory-colored bamboo shoots in Chinese groceries, but do not mistake these for fresh bamboo shoots—they have been cooked. With the hope that we can soon buy fresh bamboo shoots, I include them here.

Nearly all of the bamboo shoots we eat come ready to use in cans. There are many different kinds and sizes marketed, but they generally fall into two major categories—spring shoots and winter shoots. Although there are differences in taste, they are so subtle as to be almost undetectable. The winter shoots are smaller and considered more choice.

When I have seen fresh bamboo shoots, they were usually the large spring shoots. They look like a thick shoot, almost tusklike, measuring 3 to 5 inches in diameter at the base and tapering to a greenish point. The whole shoot can be up to 10 inches in length. The coarse outer leaves are tightly wrapped around the shoot, and they may have a pinkish tinge at the base. Fresh bamboo shoots are crunchier and sweeter than the canned variety.

How to Use
Fresh bamboo shoots contain a bitter toxin, hydrocyanic acid, so they *must* be parboiled before cooking. Canned shoots have obviously been treated and are ready to use, although a thorough rinse in warm water is recommended. The coarse outer leaves should be removed, the base cut off and discarded. The central core is what is edible. Slice or cut into the desired size and parboil in rapidly boiling water for 5 minutes. Drain, refresh, and taste. If the shoots taste bitter, repeat the parboiling process before using. Bamboo shoots are good stir-fried, stewed, braised, and cut up, and added to rice, ground meat, soups, noodles, and vegetarian dishes. As their taste is mild, they blend well with many flavors.

Storage and Care

Canned or fresh parboiled shoots should be stored in water to which a few grains of salt have been added, then the container covered and kept in the refrigerator. The shoots will keep for weeks if the water is changed every four or five days. Although they can be frozen, I do not recommend this, as the shoots tend to become soft and spongy.

Cultivation Tips

Not feasible for the home gardener.

Bamboo Shoots with Chard Ribbons

Yields 4 servings

This simple dish contrasts the crunchy bamboo with the soft, wilted green ribbons of chard. It makes a nice color contrast as well. Although the recipe calls for the bamboo shoots to be cut into strips, if the ones you buy are already sliced, you can use them just as they are.

> 2 cups canned bamboo shoots (*chuk sun*), rinsed in warm water
> 1 pound Swiss chard
> 1 tablespoon vegetable oil
> 1 garlic clove, minced
> 1 teaspoon minced fresh ginger
> 2 tablespoons scallion, green and white parts minced
> 1 1/2 tablespoons thin soy sauce
> 2 tablespoons sherry
> 3/4 cup unsalted or low-sodium chicken stock
> 1/4 teaspoon sugar
> 1 teaspoon cornstarch, mixed with 1 tablespoon cold water
> 1 teaspoon roasted sesame oil

If using whole bamboo shoots, slice and cut into matchsticks. Wash the chard, remove stems, and reserve for another use. Pile the leaves and cut into ribbons about 1/4 inch wide.

In a wok, heat the oil. Add the garlic, ginger, and scallion, and stir-fry until aromatic, about 30 seconds. Add the bamboo shoots, stir-fry 1 minute, then add the chard ribbons and continue tossing another minute.

Add the soy sauce, sherry, stock, and sugar. Stir to blend, turn down the heat, and cook until the chard ribbons are soft and wilted, 3 to 5 minutes. Add the cornstarch mixture, bring to a boil, and simmer until sauce thickens and coats the vegetables. Remove from heat, drizzle with sesame oil, and serve.

Winter Bamboo Shoots

3

Herbs

Scallions
Tsung · Cong
Allium fistulosum

Several years ago, when my dear friend Marcella Hazan was in New York, she mentioned she would like to buy a wok to take back to Venice. I volunteered to go to Chinatown with her, and said that she could probably stock up quite well on canned, salted, and dried ingredients to produce authentic Chinese food, but that she would need fresh ginger, garlic, and scallions. Ginger and garlic, Marcella said, were no problem. It was the scallions that were nowhere to be found in Italy.

Fresh scallions, also called spring onions, bunching onions, and Welsh onions, are an indispensable ingredient in Chinese cooking. They are native to Asia and have been used in Chinese cooking for hundreds of years. For authentic flavor, there is no substitute. I tried using the green parts of sprouting onions when I lived in Europe, but they were never quite the same. These slender green onions are no more than 1/2 inch thick and 8 to 10 inches long. They are about one-third white stem and two-thirds hollow green leaf. They taste of onion, but are milder and sweeter, and are used in all Asian cuisines as a seasoning vegetable. Together with ginger and garlic, they are the *mirepoix* of Asian cuisine.

How to Use
Both white and green parts of scallions are used. They can be minced, cut into various lengths, or used whole. Use as a seasoning vegetable for stir-fries, by themselves or in combination with ginger and garlic. Scallions are used with all meats, fish, seafood, and poultry, in soups, braises, stews, and even grilled. They are never served alone as a vegetable in Asian cuisines.

Storage and Care
Look for fresh green scallions, usually sold tied in bunches, with a little of the roots on, as these will stay fresh longest. Store in a plastic bag in the vegetable bin of the refrigerator. They should keep a week or longer. Trim and wash before use.

Cultivation Tips
Scallions, spring onions, bunching onions, and Welsh onions are all names listed in seed catalogs. They are winter hardy although usually

grown as an annual. Varieties can be multi- or single stem. Plant in fertile, well-drained soil with a neutral pH. They can be sown in situ in spring, or large clumps from the previous season can be divided. Plants should be harvested young, in 30 or 40 days, or when they are about 6 inches high.

Scallion Crepes with Roast Duck Filling

Yields 10 main-course servings

Fresh scallions are the ingredient that makes most dishes taste authentically Chinese. In this recipe, I have married classic crepes with this ingredient. Of course, the crepes can be filled with anything savory, but this recipe uses roasted duck from Chinatown, which makes preparation easy and quick. I like to make the crepes large, about 9 inches across, so I can form soft spring rolls for a main course when served on a mound of lettuce or cucumber shreds. The crepes can also be made smaller and served as appetizers. Like most crepes, these keep well refrigerated, so they can be made well in advance. A little hoisin sauce mixed with a few drops of sesame oil makes a nice sauce to serve on the side.

> 6 scallions (*tsung*)
> 4 tablespoons butter
> 4 eggs
> 2 cups milk
> 1 teaspoon salt
> $1/2$ teaspoon freshly ground black pepper
> 2 cups all-purpose flour
>
> FOR THE FILLING:
> 1 Chinese roast duck, about 3 to 4 pounds
> 2 tablespoons lime juice
> $1/4$ cup plum wine
> 2 tablespoons roasted sesame oil
> 1 teaspoon hot chili oil
> 2 teaspoons thin soy sauce
> 1 teaspoon minced fresh ginger

Mince both green and white parts of the scallions and set aside. Melt the butter in a small saucepan; set aside.

Quick method: Combine the eggs, milk, $1/4$ cup cold water, salt, and pepper in a blender. Process to mix well. Add the flour and blend to a smooth batter. Pour in the melted butter and mix. Remove from blender to a bowl or measuring cup and stir in the minced scallions.

Hand method: In a mixing bowl or measuring cup, combine the eggs, milk, $1/4$ cup cold water, salt, and pepper. Stir to mix well. Place the flour in a bowl and make a well in the center. Gradually pour in the liquid and stir with a whisk, incorporating the flour to form a smooth batter. Stir in melted butter and scallions.

Lightly grease a 9-inch skillet or crepe pan with oil or butter. Heat pan over medium heat about 30 seconds to 1 minute. With a ¼ cup measure, pour in batter and quickly swirl the pan to form a thin crepe. Cook until top is set and bottom lightly browned, about 3 minutes. Turn the crepe and cook another minute. Slide onto a wax paper-lined plate. Repeat to form ten crepes.

To store, wrap well in wax paper and place in a plastic bag in the refrigerator. Return to room temperature or warm in a low oven, wrapped in foil, before serving.

Preheat the oven to 400°F.

For the filling, remove the skin and meat from the duck. Separate the skin from meat, and cut the skin into large pieces, and place on a baking sheet. Sliver the duck meat and place in a bowl. Crisp the skin in a hot oven for 5 minutes. The meat can be warmed slightly as well, or left at room temperature.

In a small saucepan, whisk together the lime juice, plum wine, sesame oil, chili oil, soy sauce, and ginger. Bring to a simmer and cook gently until hot. Pour over the duck meat. Toss to blend and use to fill the pancakes. Pancakes may be filled individually at the table by diners or the spring rolls can be prepared ahead. Garnish with pieces of crisp skin.

Cilantro
Yuen Sai · Yuan Qian
Coriandrum sativum

This is one herb that people either love or hate—there doesn't seem to be a middle ground. It is also known as fresh coriander or Chinese parsley.

Dried coriander seeds and fresh coriander leaves were part of the cuisines of ancient Egypt and Rome. The herb was introduced to Asia by early traders, and it has remained popular to this day. The most common name for fresh coriander—cilantro—is its Spanish name because this herb is also important in Mexican cooking. The Thai use this fragrant herb—its roots, stems, and leaves—to flavor their dishes generously; indeed, cilantro is popular throughout Southeast Asia. It is also used in Indian cuisine. The Chinese, especially the Cantonese, use cilantro mostly as a garnish, generously strewn over steamed whole fish, and in soups, although it is often used in dumpling fillings. The only Asian country where cilantro is not popular is Japan.

Cilantro is available almost everywhere today, but I like to buy it best from Asian markets because they always sell the herb with its roots intact. This is the best way to buy cilantro, as it is delicate and wilts very easily. Even with the roots cut off, cilantro usually comes as a cluster of stalks and leaves still joined at the base. The bright green leaves are indented and look like feathery parsley. Cilantro has a strong, distinctive earthy taste, and if used with too generous a hand tends to taste a bit soapy. It is important to remember that coriander seeds—whole or ground—do not taste the same as the fresh leaves and cannot be used as a substitute.

How to Use
All of the cilantro plant—roots, stems, and leaves—can be used, and many Thai recipes call for the roots. If not using the roots, cut off and discard. Separate the stalks and discard if not required. Cilantro tends to be gritty, so it is best to immerse it in several changes of cold water. Feathery cilantro makes a beautiful garnish strewn over fish, on top of salads, and added to soups at the last minute. It is often chopped up and added to dressings and sauces, and can be used in fresh rice rolls in place of mint.

Storage and Care
Whenever possible, buy cilantro with roots attached. Wrap the roots in a damp paper towel and put the bundle in an open plastic bag, and

store in the vegetable bin of the refrigerator. If the cilantro is fresh, it will keep very well this way for a week or longer. Do not wash cilantro until ready to use, and avoid leaving it standing in water too long as it can become waterlogged. Once this herb wilts, it cannot be brought back.

Cultivation Tips

Grow cilantro from seed much as you would chervil or parsley. It matures within a few weeks and goes to seed rapidly, so for a cutting supply throughout the season, sow it several times.

Cilantro Pesto

Yields ½ cup

Fresh cilantro is used in many Asian cuisines, but this herb is very fragile, and even growing it doesn't quite help if you always want some on hand, as the plant goes to seed very fast. Besides providing you with a sauce, turning it into pesto makes it possible to use fresh cilantro before it has to be thrown out. The sauce is versatile enough, so you can add it to soups, broths, curries, and mayonnaise—or use just as you would basil pesto.

> 2 cups loosely packed fresh cilantro leaves (*yuen sai*)
> 2 garlic cloves
> ¼ cup pine nuts, toasted
> 2 tablespoons extra-virgin olive oil
> ¼ cup vegetable oil
> 1 teaspoon salt
> 1 tablespoon rice vinegar

In a blender or food processor, pulse together the cilantro, garlic, and pine nuts until coarsely chopped. Drizzle in the olive oil and vegetable oil and continue processing until smooth. Add the salt and rice vinegar and pulse to blend well. Use immediately or store in a covered glass jar, refrigerated.

Note: For cilantro pesto mayonnaise, mix equal parts of Cilantro Pesto and mayonnaise. If you wish to add this to a soup, dilute the mayonnaise with an equal amount of hot soup, whisking until the mayonnaise is completely smooth before adding to the broth, or the mixture will be lumpy.

Garlic Chives, Yellow Chives, Flowering Garlic Chives

Gau Choy, Gau Wong, Gau Choy Fa (Gau Choy Sum) · Jiu Cai, Jiu Huang, Jiu Cai Hua

Allium tuberosum

韭菜

韭黃

韭菜花

Garlic chives (also called Chinese chives) differ from regular chives in that the leaves are flat, like green linguine, and the plant is larger and more robust. The plant is used in three forms by the Chinese: the green-leaved plant; the same plant grown in the dark, or blanched, to keep the leaves white or yellow; and the chive flowers, which are really buds. All three forms have a mild garlic flavor and are used abundantly as a vegetable, not sparingly as an herb. The leaves— green or yellow—are 8 to 10 inches long and $1/4$ inch wide. The shorter leaves are supposed to be younger and more tender. The dark green plants are sold tied in bunches, and the yellow or blanched plants are sold in limp piles.

In China, the green plants traditionally are covered with straw cupolas or special clay pots to keep them in the dark and prevent the chlorophyll from developing, thus forcing the leaves to remain pale yellow. Blanching weakens the plant, so it is typically done after some green chive leaves have been harvested, which may be more than once a year, depending on climate. The commercial blanching process is far less picturesque, as this is done on a large scale, and involves covering the plants with sheets of black plastic.

Garlic chive flowers—really a misnomer, as these are usually buds— have tubular stems about 8 inches long, with an oval bud at the top. They are sold as a separate, more expensive, vegetable, tied into small bunches about 2 inches thick. Although the flowers are also edible and pretty, the Chinese never allow the buds to open for eating purposes.

When young and fresh, all three forms of garlic chives have an oniony, honeylike flavor and a delicate aroma. As they age the aroma becomes pungent and the flavor intensifies. Green garlic chives are normally available in Asian markets almost year-round, although the buds and yellow chives are more prevalent in warmer months.

How to Use

Green garlic chives are used in stir-fries with meat, liver (great!), poultry, bean curd, and noodles; in soups; scrambled with eggs; in dumplings; and even deep-fried. The flowers are used in the same way, but more sparingly owing to cost. Yellow chives, being soft and pricier,

are most often put in soups and steamed dishes, although they could also be used in any of the ways that green chive leaves are used. Keep bunches tied together for easy handling, rinse well in cold water, cut off whitish stems and tips, and cut into desired lengths for cooking.

Storage and Care

Green garlic chives—leaves and flowers—should be placed in a brown paper bag and stored in the vegetable bin of the refrigerator. They will keep about one week, but the smell becomes very strong. Yellow chives are stored in the same way, but should be used within two days. Try to keep chives as dry as possible.

Cultivation Tips

Garlic chives are easy to grow. Several seed catalogs list the tiny dark seeds. Old seeds do not germinate easily, so be sure to use fresh ones. As with other chives, sow seed outdoors in spring, after all danger of frost, in moist, rich soil with full sun. Cut back often to keep the plants from going yellow, and do not overfeed. Plants grow to 18 inches high, producing buds that open into small umbrella-shaped white flowers.

This hardy plant is frost and disease resistant, and in warm climates will stay green over winter. Enthusiasts may wish to cultivate these plants indoors year-round in a sunny window.

Garlic Chive Dumplings

Yields 36 dumplings

I love these delicious dumplings, which are a new variation on the delicate *har kow* shrimp dumplings that are basic dim sum cuisine. In this recipe, I use scallops instead of the more ordinary shrimp version you find in restaurants. Leftover dumplings can be frozen after they are cooked and reheated without defrosting.

    2 cups green garlic chives (*gau choy*), about 6 ounces
    2 tablespoons plus 2 teaspoons vegetable oil
    2 teaspoons thin soy sauce
    1/2 teaspoon freshly ground black pepper
    1 teaspoon roasted sesame oil
    2 teaspoons cornstarch, mixed with 2 tablespoons cold water
    1 package wonton skins
    36 bay scallops
    Napa cabbage leaves to line bamboo steamer

Cut the garlic chives into 1/4-inch pieces. In a small skillet, heat 2 teaspoons of the oil over medium heat. Add the chives and sauté until

Flowering Garlic Chives

wilted, about 30 seconds. Add the soy sauce, pepper, sesame oil, and cornstarch mixture. Cook until thickened, stirring often, about 1 minute. Remove from heat and cool.

Use a pair of scissors or a round biscuit cutter to cut the wonton skins into 2½-inch circles.

Place 1 teaspoon chive mixture in the center of each circle and press 1 scallop into mixture. Moisten edges with water, pleat half the circle, press edges together, and seal to form a crescent-shaped dumpling. Alternatively, pleat around in a circle and press edges together to form a beggar's purse. Repeat to form 36 dumplings.

Line a 9- or 10-inch bamboo steamer basket with cabbage leaves and place in a wok or deep-sided skillet filled with enough water to touch the bottom of the basket. Cover and steam 3 to 5 minutes to wilt the cabbage leaves slightly. Arrange the dumplings on the leaves and steam until translucent, 5 to 8 minutes. Serve warm with a soy sauce and vinegar dip and hot chili sauce.

Yellow Chives and Salmon in Rice Paper Packets

Yields 6 servings

Yellow chives are so special that I present a recipe that, although a little troublesome, is interesting, beautiful, and delicious! Serving these packets on a bed of watercress sauce will draw raves!

> 2 cups loosely packed yellow chives (*gau wong*), about 6 ounces
> 3 tablespoons unsalted butter
> 6 10-inch round sheets of rice paper
> 1½ pounds salmon fillet, about 1 inch thick
> 2 teaspoons fresh thyme leaves
> 1 tablespoon freshly ground black pepper
> 2 teaspoons salt
> 2 tablespoons dry white wine
> 2 tablespoons fresh lemon juice
> Watercress Sauce (page 63)
> Chives flowers, for garnish

Rinse the yellow chives, trim if necessary, and cut into 4-inch lengths.

In a skillet, over medium heat, melt the butter and sauté the chives until wilted, about 1 minute. Set aside and let cool.

Dip the rice papers in a bowl of warm water and lay out on a clean dish towel. Cut the salmon into 6 equal pieces.

Chop the thyme leaves and combine with pepper and salt. Sprinkle over fish. Divide the chives into 6 equal portions and place 1 portion in the center of each rice paper sheet. Arrange a piece of salmon

Garlic Chives

over each mound of chives, drizzle the fish pieces with wine and lemon juice, then fold the rice paper into a rectangular packet. Repeat until 6 packets are formed. Place 3 packets seam-side down on each of two 8- or 9-inch plates that will fit your bamboo steaming baskets.

Set the plates in 2 tiers of a bamboo steamer basket. Place in a wok or deep skillet filled with enough water to cover the bottom of the lower basket by about ½ inch. Over medium heat, steam the fish until just done and slightly rare in the center, 12 to 15 minutes.

To serve, cover the center of each plate with some sauce, and lay a fish packet in the center. Garnish with chive flowers, if desired.

See photograph on pages 148–149.

Garlic Chive Flowers Stir-Fried with Sliced Beef

Yields 4 servings

Chive flowers turn this homey dish into something special, but green chives make a fine substitute. Yellow chives, however, are too delicate.

¾ pound flank steak

FOR THE MARINADE:
2 teaspoons cornstarch
2 teaspoons dark soy sauce
1 teaspoon minced fresh ginger

•

½ pound garlic chive flowers (*gau choy fa*)
1 tablespoon oyster sauce
2 tablespoons dry sherry
1 teaspoon sugar
¼ teaspoon freshly ground black pepper
2 tablespoons vegetable oil

Slice the flank steak across the grain into pieces about ¼ inch thick and 1 inch long. Do not be overly concerned if you have to cut the pieces a little thicker; just make sure they are uniform in size.

In a bowl, combine the steak with the cornstarch, soy sauce, and ginger for the marinade. Set aside.

Rinse garlic chive flowers under cold water. Drain. Cut into 2-inch pieces, using both stems and buds. Set aside.

Combine the oyster sauce, sherry, sugar, and pepper in a bowl.

In a wok, heat the oil over medium heat until just smoking. In two batches, stir-fry the steak until seared but pink inside, about 3 minutes per batch. Add the chives and continue stir-frying, tossing to blend well, about 1 minute or until the chives are just wilted. Add the oyster sauce mixture and cook, stirring to blend and heat through, about 30 seconds, and serve.

Yellow Chives

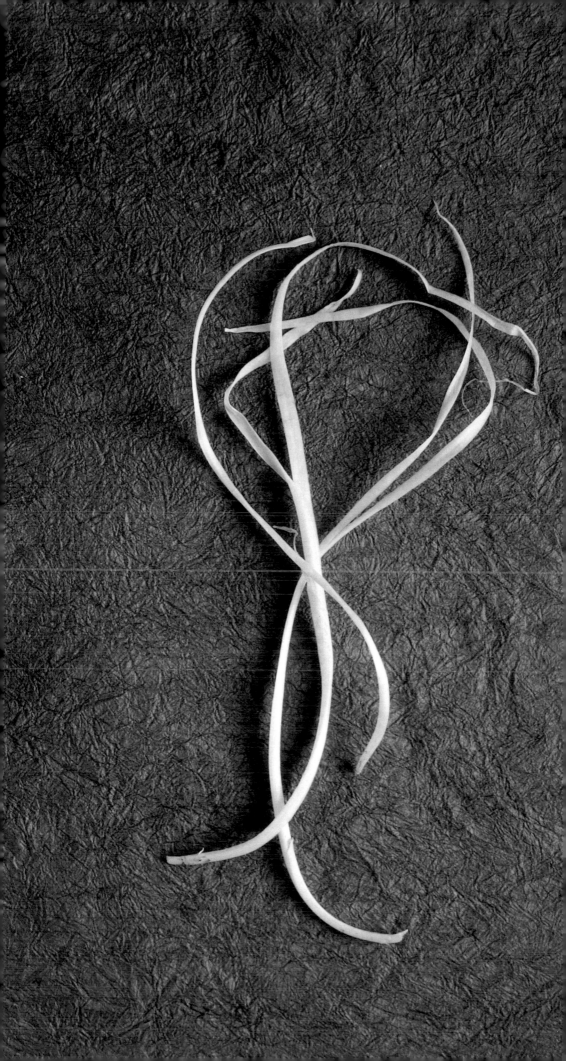

Chinese Celery
Kun Choy · Qin Cai
Apium graveolens dulce

Chinese celery is an ancient vegetable in China, and recipes for dishes using it have been found on the bamboo slips used to record recipes excavated from Han dynasty tombs. The Cantonese use Chinese celery in the vegetarian dishes they serve during Chinese New Year. A play on the Chinese words for "celery" and "diligence" suggests that eating this vegetable on the first day of the year brings an appetite for hard work that will result in success.

This celery looks like the Western kind, except that the stalks are only about ½ inch thick and the whole head usually measures only 1 to 2 inches across and about 10 inches long. The entire stalk is bright green and there are more leaves. Being a smaller version of Western celery, one would think that Chinese celery would taste more delicate, but the contrary is the case. Chinese celery is very pungent and so is seldom used raw, but it sweetens when it is cooked. Sometimes it is even blanched to mellow its flavor before it is used in a stir-fried dish.

How to Use
Cut off the base and discard. Separate the stalks and wash well. Remove the leaves, if desired, and cut stems into fine pieces or desired shapes for cooking. It is usually stir-fried with meat, poultry, vegetables, and seafood and can be used to flavor soups and rice.

Storage and Care
Keep the celery, wrapped, in the vegetable bin of the refrigerator and treat as you would regular celery. It should keep a few weeks before wilting, but even then can still be used.

Cultivation Tips
Chinese celery needs fertile conditions and soil that retains water well. It is a temperate climate plant and holds up to cold conditions fairly well. The plants grow 10 to 15 inches high; if allowed to go to seed, Chinese celery will self-sow. Although slow at first, it grows well once established and should be large enough for cutting in about six weeks. In the garden, the whole plant need not be cut, only individual stalks as needed. Unlike branch celery, Chinese celery is never blanched.

Yields 4 servings

The strong taste of this celery mellows and becomes smooth in cooking. And the bright green color is pretty in this otherwise dark-looking dish. Traditionally, the celery is cooked with pressed bean curd, but that can be difficult to find and this version is simpler.

$3/4$ pound Chinese celery (*kun choy*)
10 small dried black mushrooms
1 pound firm tofu
1 tablespoon vegetable oil
1 scallion, green and white parts minced
1 teaspoon minced fresh ginger
2 tablespoons dark soy sauce
$1/4$ teaspoon freshly ground black pepper
1 tablespoon cornstarch, mixed with 2 tablespoons cold water
A few drops roasted sesame oil

Wash and cut the celery into 2-inch pieces, discarding the leaves. You should have about $1/2$ cup. Soak the mushrooms in warm water until soft, about 15 minutes. Drain and reserve $1/2$ cup of the mushroom water. Drain the tofu and cut into $1^{1}/2$-inch cubes.

In a wok, heat the oil over medium heat. Stir-fry the celery until it turns bright green but is still crisp, about 1 minute. Remove to a plate and reserve.

Return the wok to the heat, add the scallion and ginger, and stir-fry until aromatic, about 30 seconds. Add the mushrooms, tofu cubes, soy sauce, reserved mushroom liquid, and pepper. Bring to a boil, reduce heat, and simmer 10 minutes. Add the cornstarch mixture, bring to a boil to thicken, then add the reserved celery. Cook another 3 minutes. Remove from heat, drizzle with sesame oil, and serve.

Lemongrass
Heung Mao Tso · Xiang Mao Cao
Cymbopogon citratus

My friend and colleague Katharine Alford loves lemongrass. It was no surprise, therefore, that when we planned an East-West Tea for our culinary group, we had to include lemongrass in something. Our menu was an exciting one. We had leaf-wrapped dumplings, green-tea petit fours, various kinds of tea sandwiches, tea eggs, and a luxurious open-faced smoked salmon canapé on black bread. But what made this salmon sandwich so special was the lemongrass butter that Katharine made. The citronella flavor of the lemongrass was different enough from ordinary lemon to lend an edge of mystery to our canapés.

You can easily identify these stiff grasslike stalks in the market. They are often seen standing in a little water or lying in bunches. The whiter parts of the stems are slightly swollen and end in dried green leaves that have been bluntly cut off. (At farmers' markets, the green leaves often are intact.)

Although we think of lemongrass as an Asian herb used extensively in Southeast Asia, it is known as citronella in Europe and has been in use there for centuries. Lemongrass is infused in a tea by Buddhist monks, who offer it as a soothing drink to guests. The grass has a fragrant lemon scent and delicate flavor. It does not have the tartness of lemon. When used in soups or stews, it does not disintegrate and disappear; it remains coarse, so it is best removed from a dish before serving.

How to Use

Remove the coarse outer leaves, cut off the dried green tops, and discard; only the soft white inner stem is used. Very fresh lemongrass has purple circles that are visible when the stalk is cut crosswise. They can be bruised or crushed to release more flavor, before being cut into 1- to 2-inch lengths and added to soups, stews, and curries. Lemongrass can also be finely chopped or minced, but this makes it difficult to remove after cooking. It makes a flavorful ingredient in marinades and it flavors meat, poultry, and fish dishes very well. If the fresh green leaves are available, they can be tied into a bundle and used as a bouquet garni to infuse tea, stock, and soups. Dried lemongrass is also available, but it doesn't have the aromatic qualities of the fresh.

Storage and Care

Fresh lemongrass can be kept in the refrigerator ten days or longer, depending on freshness. Do not let it get wet, as it will decay. Lemongrass can be frozen quite successfully, in which case it should be used directly from the freezer. It can be chopped and dried, although it loses almost all fragrance in this form.

Cultivation Tips

This tropical perennial grass seldom flowers, so it is best grown by planting pieces of root or subdividing clumps. In temperate areas, treat it as an annual. I have rooted lemongrass from weeks-old stalks bought at the market, simply by sticking them in fertile garden soil and watering. They grow into beautiful 3- to 5-foot clumps in one season and are ornamental as well. This plant also repels insects, so if you like the look, a few clumps planted around the garden is not a bad idea!

Lemongrass Broth

Yields about 6 cups

The delicate flavor of lemongrass is so delicious, I made this all-purpose broth as a base for soups. You can use the broth in any of the soup recipes in this book, especially the simpler ones using melons and squashes. It will add dimension to your soup. Unfortunately, most of the lemongrass flavor is lost after a few weeks if frozen.

> 6 stalks lemongrass (*heung mao tso*)
> 3 pounds chicken parts
> 2 thyme sprigs, preferably lemon thyme

Trim off the coarse outer leaves from the lemongrass stalks. Cut into 3-inch lengths, and with the flat side of a heavy knife, mash the white parts of the stalks.

Place the chicken parts in a stockpot and cover with 8 to 10 cups cold water. Bring to a boil, reduce heat, and skim surface a few times during the first 10 minutes. Add the lemongrass and thyme, and simmer stock 3 to 4 hours or until flavorful. Strain and discard chicken parts and vegetables. Cool and degrease completely before using.

Lemongrass Butter

Yields ¾ pound

Originally, my colleague and friend Katharine Alford made this butter to serve on delicate smoked salmon sandwiches. The method we used was long and tedious, and involved a piece of special equipment. The

butter was so good, however, that I came up with a simpler way of making it. Don't make too much at a time, as it won't keep very long. The butter is great spread on bread, as a topping for fish or vegetables, and even slightly sweetened and used on pancakes and waffles.

> 3 to 4 thick stalks, or 6 thin stalks, lemongrass (*heung mao tso*)
> 2 cups heavy cream (not ultrapasteurized)
> Salt

Remove the coarse stalks from the lemongrass, cut off the green tops, and discard or use in broth. With the flat side of a heavy knife, bruise the stalks and then slice thinly.

In a heavy saucepan, over very low heat, infuse the cream with the lemongrass. Barely simmer for 20 minutes or until the cream is flavored. Cover and let stand until cool. Strain into a metal dish and refrigerate until completely cold.

With a hand mixer, whip the cream until it turns to butter, 20 to 30 minutes depending on how much cream you have in the bowl. Flavor lightly with salt.

Line a strainer with dampened cheesecloth and add the butter. Let stand in the refrigerator overnight; about 1 tablespoon of liquid will "sweat" out of the butter. Wrap tightly and refrigerate. It will keep for at least 1 week.

Horapah Basil

Horapah Basil, Holy Basil, Hairy Basil
*Bai Horapah, Bai Graprao, Bai Mengluk (Thai) ·
Lo Kak, Luo Le · Dzi Sou, Zi Su*
Ocimum basilicum, O. sanctum, O. canum

The Chinese do not use basil in their cooking, so the first time I
encountered it was in Italy. We used to drive down the coast from
Milan in the summer to spend weekends at a charming fishing village
just south of Genoa. One summer afternoon, we walked into a *trattoria*
and were struck by the aromatic smell of basil, which is the basis for
the famous Genovese pesto. I have searched but have never found
basil of such perfume, and I am convinced that the Mediterranean sun
has everything to do with the aroma of Genovese basil.

The basil of pesto is sweet basil. However, when I first
encountered basil in a Thai dish, I realized there was more to learn
about this wonderful herb. The dish was listed on the menu as made
with holy basil, and I thought this was a religious allusion to an herb
that deserved a place of honor in any kitchen. Later I was to learn
about hairy basil, yet a third variety of the herb.

Basil is in the mint family, and the three varieties of basil favored
by Thai cooks, who use this herb generously in their food, are the ones
you will find in Asian markets. Indeed, basil plays a dominant role in
the kitchens of Thailand, Laos, Cambodia, and Vietnam.

The easiest variety to find is horapah basil, similar to the shiny
green-leaved Italian variety. It has a slight anise flavor and sometimes
has dark purple stems. Holy basil is commonly found only in Asian
markets frequented by immigrants from Southeast Asia, but it is
beginning to show up at farmers' markets. Its leaves are smooth but
not shiny, the edges of which are slightly serrated. Holy basil leaves
can be green or tinged with red or purple, the flavor, though not strong,
intensifies in cooking. The easiest variety to identify—but hardest to
find—is hairy, or hoary, basil. This variety has long, narrow, pale green
leaves and a strong lemon scent and a peppery flavor. The seeds are
tinged with red, and when dried can be used in drinks. The fresh
leaves are good in salads and make a pretty garnish.

How to Use
Asians use basil in soups and noodle dishes and raw in salads, much
as Westerners do. Any basil or mint can be substituted, but I tend to
use a little more than usual, depending on how aromatic the basil is.

Storage and Care

All three varieties of basil are fragile and should be used soon after purchase. The cuttings keep best when they stand in a little water, covered loosely with a plastic bag and left in the refrigerator.

Cultivation Tips

For gardeners with a green thumb, you might want to root a few sprigs of holy or hairy basil from bunches purchased at the market. Seeds for the Asian varieties are available by mail order. Grow the seedlings in a sunny location in moist, fertile soil. Pinch the tops to make bushier plants and keep them from going to seed early.

Duck Curry with Horapah Basil

Yields 4 servings

The spices in this dish will give you a yellow curry. I have made the curry a little simpler, with more accessible ingredients. The result is still delicious, and the horapah basil lends a distinctive perfume. Because duck is so fatty, I suggest making the curry well in advance, even a day ahead, cooling it, and then removing most of the congealed fat. Reheat before serving. If you like your curry really spicy, add a few more chilies or serve it with some Indonesian sambal on the side. Serve with plenty of white rice and a simple vegetable side dish.

> 1 whole fresh duck, about 5 pounds
> ¹⁄₂ cup *horapah* or sweet basil leaves, loosely packed, plus additional for garnish
>
> FOR THE CURRY MIX:
> 1 teaspoon turmeric
> ¹⁄₂ teaspoon ground coriander
> ¹⁄₂ teaspoon ground cumin
> ¹⁄₂ teaspoon ground cardamom
> 3 slices galangal, the size of a dime (see Note)
> 1 slice fresh ginger
> 2 garlic cloves
> 1 stalk lemongrass, tender white part only
> 3 dried hot chilies
>
> •
>
> 2 cups unsweetened coconut milk
> 1 cup unsalted or low-sodium chicken stock
> 3 cilantro stalks, with roots if possible, coarsely chopped
> 1 tablespoon fish sauce (*nuoc mam* or *nam pla*)
> 1 teaspoon salt, or to taste

Cut the duck into bite-size pieces. Tear the ¹⁄₂ cup basil leaves with your fingers and set aside.

Make the curry mix. In a spice grinder or blender, grind the turmeric, coriander, cumin, cardamom, galangal, ginger, garlic, lemongrass, and chilies.

In a wok or deep saucepan, lightly brown the duck pieces, skin side down. Remove to a plate and pour off excess fat. Sauté the curry mix until aromatic, stirring constantly and being careful not to burn, about 30 seconds. Return the duck to the pan, add the coconut milk, stock, cilantro, fish sauce, salt, and torn basil leaves. Bring to a boil, reduce the heat, and simmer until the duck is tender, about 1 hour. If the duck dries out too much, add a little water.

Degrease as suggested. Just before serving, throw the handful of basil leaves into the hot curry and serve.

Holy Basil, Chicken, Shrimp, and Noodles

Yields 2 to 4 servings

It is best to use the linguine-size rice stick noodles for this dish. They absorb the delicious sauce from the stir-fry. If you really like this basil, use a little more of it than specified in the recipe. It is very delicate and loses its flavor fast, so you may want to use it more generously.

> 8 ounces rice stick noodles
> 1 cup tightly packed holy basil or sweet basil leaves (*graprao*)
> 2 tablespoons vegetable oil
> 1 stalk lemongrass, tender white part only, thinly sliced
> 2 garlic cloves, minced
> 1½ teaspoons minced galangal (see Note), or 2 teaspoons minced
>   fresh ginger
> ½ pound boneless, skinless chicken breasts, thinly sliced
> ½ pound medium shrimp, peeled and deveined
> 3 tablespoons fish sauce (*nuoc mam* or *nam pla*)
> 1 teaspoon sugar
> 4 fresh chilies, such as serrano or jalapeño
> Juice of 1 lime

Soak the rice stick noodles in hot water and let stand until white and soft, 20 to 30 minutes. Drain and reserve. Tear the basil leaves into 3 or 4 pieces per leaf and set aside.

In a wok, heat the oil, add the lemongrass, and stir-fry 10 seconds, then add the garlic, galangal, or ginger and stir-fry another 10 seconds. Add the chicken and shrimp and stir-fry, tossing constantly until chicken just turns white and shrimp pink, 5 to 8 minutes. Add the basil and toss to wilt. Add the fish sauce, sugar, chilies, and lime juice, toss to blend, then add the drained noodles. Lower the heat and cook until the noodles are soft and have absorbed nearly all the flavor.

Holy Basil

Shiso
Zi Su · Zi Su
Perilla frutescens crispa

Although the ancient Chinese used shiso leaves in cooking, today this herb is almost exclusively Japanese. You can usually find it in Japanese markets, in neat piles, carefully wrapped in plastic. Also called perilla, shiso resembles a large, flat parsley leaf with sharply serrated edges, measuring 2 inches across at the widest. The leaves are lighter green than parsley, and the flavor has a hint of licorice, mint, or cinnamon—depending on your taste buds. There is a red-leaved type and varieties that are tinged with more or less red and bronze, but the green variety has the strongest flavor and is the common one.

How to Use
The Japanese use shiso with fish or meat, raw in salads, pickled alone or with other fruit, and as a garnish. It can be deep-fried as tempura, or used to flavor barbecues, soups, and rice and potato dishes. The red variety colors food pink.

Storage and Care
Use fresh shiso leaves within 2 days of purchase. Store well wrapped in the refrigerator.

Cultivation Tips
You may have to do some searching, but shiso seeds can be ordered from some Asian seed houses. This tender annual herb is not difficult to grow and can generally be treated much like basil. It thrives in acid soil in climates with average temperatures in the mid-60s. The bushy plants grow to two feet. Shiso also makes a good container herb.

Shiso Beurre Blanc

Yields approximately ½ cup

This Japanese herb has a tart, minty flavor. It is most often served raw in a sushi roll with sour umeboshi pickled plums. I thought the flavor worked well in this beurre blanc, which is great poured over some simply poached sea scallops.

> ¼ cup rice vinegar
> ¼ cup dry white wine
> 1 tablespoon minced shallot

5 shiso leaves (*zi su*), cut into very fine ribbons
$^1/_2$ pound cold butter, cut into cubes
$^1/_2$ teaspoon salt
$^1/_4$ teaspoon freshly ground black pepper

In a nonreactive saucepan, combine the vinegar, wine, shallot, and shiso shreds. Bring to a boil and cook until the liquid reduces to 1 tablespoon.

Turn the heat down very low and bit by bit, whisk in the butter, being careful not to let the sauce get too hot or the butter will separate. You want to achieve a creamy emulsion. When all the butter is used up, remove from heat. Season with salt and pepper, and serve immediately.

Note: If you must make a beurre blanc in advance, the easiest way to hold it is in a thermos bottle. You can also wrap a kitchen towel around the bowl and set it in a pan of hot, but not boiling, water.

Shiso Risotto

Yields 4 main-course or 6 side-dish servings

Shiso flavors rice beautifully, and as risotto is one of my favorite dishes, I find this combination to be very tasty. A sprinkling of Parme san cheese works very well. The rice can be served by itself, with fresh peas or sugar snaps folded in at the last five minutes. Lobster, scallops, or shrimp stirred in will turn it into an exotic seafood risotto.

2 tablespoons butter, plus 1 to 2 tablespoons (optional) to fold in

at the end
1 cup minced onion
5 shiso leaves (*zi su*), coarsely chopped
$1^1/_2$ cups arborio rice
$4^1/_2$ to 5 cups unsalted or low-sodium chicken stock, kept at a simmer
$^1/_2$ teaspoon salt
$^1/_4$ teaspoon freshly ground black pepper

In a heavy saucepan, over medium heat, melt the 2 tablespoons but ter, add the onion, and sauté until wilted, about 5 minutes. Add the shiso and stir once or twice, then add the rice and stir until well coated with the butter.

One or two ladlefuls at a time, add the simmering broth, turning the rice constantly with a wooden spoon. When the broth is absorbed, repeat a little at a time, until each grain of rice is cooked completely through, but not falling apart. A good risotto should have a creamy consistency. The process takes 25 to 30 minutes.

Fold in the extra butter, if desired, and serve at once.

Burdock

Burdock
Gobo (Japanese) · Ngao Pong · Niu Bang
Arctium lappa

Most New Yorkers have come to love the greenmarkets, set up in various locations in the city several days a week. The farmers can be counted on to introduce new and exotic vegetables and fruits. Once, I was intrigued by a long, dark root and was told that it was edible burdock. Up until then I knew this vegetable only as a Japanese pickle. I discovered that although burdock has been used in China since ancient times for medicinal purposes, the Japanese regard it as a delicacy. Burdock was introduced to Europe through France in the 1870s, and reached North America shortly thereafter, where it is considered a weed. In Japan, it is called *gobo*.

Fresh burdock root is not a common vegetable, but when available you can recognize the dark brown tapering roots that can be as long as 4 feet and 1 inch wide. Beneath the dark skin is white flesh that discolors easily when exposed to oxygen. Burdock tastes sweetly mild when young, but the flavor intensifies as the root becomes woody with age. It snaps easily when bent, so the roots are often in pieces when you buy them. When eaten raw, very young roots have a crisp fresh taste, but burdock is usually cooked. Pickled pencil-thin pieces of burdock, orange in color, are readily available packaged in Asian groceries.

How to Use
Burdock should be lightly peeled, as the part just beneath the skin is the sweetest. The white flesh should be soaked in cold or acidulated water for about an hour to remove bitterness. It is best parboiled until tender, then stir-fried, boiled, roasted, or stewed by itself or with other root vegetables. Burdock is often pickled with rice vinegar.

Storage and Care
Store the roots wrapped in paper in the refrigerator for about one week.

Cultivation Tips
Look for burdock seeds in Asian seed catalogs. This hardy plant is grown as an annual and seeds can be sown in spring and autumn in warm humid areas. Burdock likes deep sandy loams with good drainage. When soil conditions are less than ideal, it is often planted

Herbs

on ridges. Prepare the site with bonemeal or other high-phosphate fertilizer. Established plants can be mulched to minimize weeding and flowering shoots should be pinched off. Spring seedlings will be ready for harvesting in four to five months. Autumn plants must overwinter and will be ready the following summer.

Burdock Simply Sautéed

Yields 2 servings

This root is most commonly pickled and is often colored orange. When peeling the root, do so very quickly and plunge the pieces immediately into acidulated water, as burdock discolors rapidly.

> 2 lemons
> ½ pound burdock (*ngao pong*)
> 1 tablespoon butter
> 2 shiso leaves or 2 parsley sprigs, coarsely chopped
> 1 teaspoon dark soy sauce
> Pinch of sugar

Cut the lemons in half and squeeze into a bowl of cold water for acidulated water. Peel the burdock, slice very quickly, and plunge into the water as you work. Let burdock soak for 1 hour. Drain.

In a saucepan, cover the burdock with fresh water, bring to a boil, reduce heat, and simmer until tender, about 45 minutes. Drain.

Melt the butter in a skillet, toss in the burdock and shiso leaves or parsley, and sauté 1 or 2 minutes. Add the soy sauce and a pinch of sugar. Stir to coat and flavor and serve.

Tamarind
Asam Koh (Indonesian) · Lo Mog Dzi · Lo Wang Zi
Tamarindus indica

My roots are in Macao, and the cuisine there included elements from many cultures, primarily Chinese and Portuguese. One of my family's favorite dishes was cross cultural before that became the vogue: pork with tamarind and shrimp paste. The sour taste of the tamarind fruit combines well with the rich pork in its equally rich sauce.

In Asian markets, you will see large dark pods that look a bit like broad beans. This is the fruit of the tamarind tree. In fact, this is not the best way to buy tamarind, as the flesh in the pods is sticky and fibrous and has to be scraped out, then soaked and separated—a tiresome and time-consuming way to acquire a tablespoon of tamarind pulp. There is little advantage to using the fresh pulp, as there is no loss of flavor in processing. Happily, tamarind pulp can be bought in blocks or in a concentrated paste, which is infinitely more practical.

Besides being used as an ingredient in cooking, tamarind seeds are made into sweets, tamarind pulp is made into chutney, and a delicious sweet-tart drink can be made from the paste. It acts as a tenderizer as well as a flavoring for meats. A mild laxative, tamarind is considered cooling to the system, and is good for the liver and kidneys.

How to Use
Small pieces of tamarind pulp should be soaked in warm water before being added to gravies, curries, soups, and marinades. The concentrated paste is easily spooned out, but then has to be soaked to separate the pulp from the fibers and seeds.

Storage and Care
Fresh pods should be used within a week. Pulp in blocks or concentrate can be stored at room temperature in a sealed container, and it will keep for months. All pulp, fresh or dried, must be soaked in warm water before use. The soaking water can usually be added to the dish. Any unused pulp should be refrigerated in a covered container.

Cultivation Tips
Not applicable.

Yields 4 servings

Lamb shanks are economical and popular. These Asian flavorings bring a new twist to an old-fashioned dish. I serve them with Shiso Risotto (page 178) and slightly bitter, acidy mizuna (see page 34), which balances the richness of the shanks.

> $^1/_2$ cup tamarind pulp (*asam koh*), about 4 ounces
> 4 meaty lamb shanks, about $^3/_4$ to 1 pound each
> 1 teaspoon salt
> 1 teaspoon freshly ground black pepper
> 2 tablespoons vegetable oil
> 2 scallions, green and white parts minced
> 2 teaspoons minced fresh ginger
> 2 garlic cloves, minced
> $^1/_4$ cup dark soy sauce
> 2 tablespoons brown sugar
> 3 dried chilies

Break up the tamarind pulp and soak in 2 cups hot water until soft, about 30 minutes. Pour through a strainer and push as much of the pulp through as possible. Discard seeds and strings. Reserve.

Sprinkle the lamb shanks with salt and pepper.

In a heavy pot, heat the oil and brown the lamb shanks, turning often. Remove to a plate. Add the scallions, ginger, and garlic and cook until aromatic, about 30 seconds. Return the lamb shanks to the pot and add the tamarind water, soy sauce, brown sugar, and chilies. Bring to a boil, turn the heat to low, and simmer with the cover askew until the lamb is tender, about 2 hours. If the sauce becomes too dry, add a little water. Turn the shanks often during cooking. Serve hot.

This dish keeps well and can be made a day in advance.

Conversion Chart

Volume Equivalents

These are not exact equivalents for the American cups and spoons, but have been rounded up or down slightly to make measuring easier.

American	Metric	Imperial
¼ t	1.25 ml	
½ t	2.5 ml	
1 t	5 ml	
½ T (1½ t)	7.5 ml	
1 T (3 t)	15 ml	
¼ cup (4 T)	60 ml	2 fl oz
⅓ cup (5 T)	75 ml	2½ fl oz
½ cup (8 T)	125 ml	4 fl oz
⅔ cup (10 T)	150 ml	5 fl oz (¼ pint)
¾ cup (12 T)	175 ml	6 fl oz (⅓ pint)
1 cup (16 T)	250 ml	8 fl oz
1¼ cups	300 ml	10 fl oz (½ pint)
1½ cups	350 ml	12 fl oz
1 pint (2 cups)	500 ml	16 fl oz
2½ cups	575 ml	20 fl oz (1 pint)
1 quart (4 cups)	1 litre	1¾ pints

Weight Equivalents

The metric weights given in this chart are not exact equivalents, but have been rounded up or down slightly to make measuring easier.

Avoirdupois	Metric
¼ oz	7 g
½ oz	15 g
1 oz	30 g
2 oz	60 g
3 oz	90 g
4 oz	115 g
5 oz	150 g
6 oz	175 g
7 oz	200 g
8 oz (½ lb)	225 g
9 oz	250 g
10 oz	300 g
11 oz	325 g
12 oz	350 g
13 oz	375 g
14 oz	400 g
15 oz	425 g
16 oz (1 lb)	450 g
1 lb 2 oz	500 g
1½ lb	750 g
2 lb	900 g
2¼ lb	1 kg
3 lb	1.4 kg
4 lb	1.8 kg
4½ lb	2 kg

Oven Temperature Equivalents

Oven	°F	°C	Gas Mark
very cool	250–275	130–140	½–1
cool	300	150	2
warm	325	170	3
moderate	350	180	4
moderately hot	375	190	5
	400	200	6
hot	425	220	7
very hot	450	230	8
	475	250	9

Acknowledgments

Writing a book is never easy and a lot of the time is spent in solitary endeavor. Despite this, a book is never solely the work of the author, and a book as beautiful as this could only happen with the help of many wonderful people.

My heartfelt thanks must go first to my editor, Ann ffolliott, who worked with me in the kindest and most generous way, and who was always there with her unstinting support and suggestions, which only improved the work; to Artisan Publisher Leslie Stoker, for her vision in mapping out a definitive guidebook that isn't dull or boring; and of course, to Peter Workman, without whose approval and backing nothing could have moved forward.

My thanks also to my wonderful, calm, and easy-going photographer, Marty Jacobs, who was never stressed over the months of photography as these vegetables went in and out of season. The resulting pictures are of unequaled beauty and they contribute so much to the book. I would also like to thank his wife, Linda Johnson, whose beautiful props and dishes were everything I had hoped for. My profound thanks also goes to my dearest friend, Paul Grimes, who suggested that I speak to Artisan at the perfect time, who was always there for advice and consultation, and who rushed in at the eleventh hour to style the food with his artist's eye.

A round vote of thanks to all at Artisan: to Jim Wageman, whose design is not only beautiful but eminently practical; to Laura Lindgren, who carried out the design; to Katya Popova and Siobhan McGowan, whose efforts helped bring the book to completion; to Hope Koturo, who made sure that production proceeded on time and with a minimum of hitches, despite many last minute additions and subtractions; to Eliza Kunkel, for her support of the book; and to Beth Wareham, who planned and executed all the publicity efforts with great thoughtfulness.

I am grateful to Carole Berglie, who copyedited the manuscript; to Cathy Dorsey, who indexed the book so thoroughly, a job I couldn't begin, much less finish; to Zhang Ying, our Chinese proofreader; to Jackie Mitchell and Ed Schneider, who gave invaluable advice on the correct Chinese terms and characters and other culinary matters.

This book would not have been started without the perseverance of my agent, Elise Goodman, who went beyond what was expected with her meticulous advice, loving kindness, and understanding when it was most needed. My cooking colleagues and friends, Nick Malgieri, Anna Amendolara Nurse, Whitney Clay, and Clayton Cooke, were always available for advice, testing, and tasting, and they made this project such fun. My Chinatown connection, Una Chang, a dear friend from childhood days in Hong Kong, was tireless in her quest for anything I needed from her contacts in the Chinese community. My daughters, Sarah and Samantha, my son-in-law Chris, all my other friends, too many to name, who tasted enthusiastically and critiqued all the recipes in the book, all deserve a big thank you. And lastly, I must thank my husband Ron, who created the special circumstances that gave me the isolation to finish this book on time. I also wish to thank Walter Gaipa of Marion Gardens Nursery who planted vegetables last summer for me to experiment with and Frederick Lee of Sang Lee Farms who provided us with perfect vegetables for photography and invaluable advice. Maria Fredericks deserves a special thank you for hunting out and sending us vegetables from California to finish our photographs.

—*East Marion, New York   June 1995*

Seed Sources

Burpee
300 Park Avenue
Warminster, PA 18974
TEL: 800-888-1447
FAX: 800-487-5530

The Cook's Garden
P.O. Box 535
Londonderry, VT 05148
TEL: 802-824-3400
FAX: 802-824-3027

Johnny's Selected Seeds
Foss Hill Road
Albion, Maine 04910-9731
TEL: 207-437-4301

Nichols Garden Nursery
1190 North Pacific Highway
Albany, OR 97321-4580
TEL: 503-928-9280
FAX: 503-967-8406

Bountiful Gardens Seeds
18001 Shafer Ranch Road
Willits, CA 95490
TEL: 707-459-6410

Oriental Seed Catalog
P.O. Box 1960
Chesterfield, VA 23832
TEL: 804-796-5796
FAX: 804-796-6735

Shepherd's Garden Seeds
30 Irene St.
Torrington, CT 06790
TEL: 203-482-3638

Stokes Seeds, Inc.
Box 548
Buffalo, NY 14240-0548
TEL: 716-695-6980
FAX: 716-695-9649

Thompson & Morgan Inc.
P.O Box 1308
Jackson, NJ 08527-0308
TEL: 800-274-7333
FAX: 908-363-9356

Vermont Bean Seed Co.
Garden Lane
Fair Haven, VT 05743
TEL: 803-663-6276
FAX: 803-663-9771

Bibliography

Chang, K.C. *Food in Chinese Culture.* New Haven: Yale University Press, 1977.

Coyle, L. Patrick. *World Encyclopedia of Food.* New York: Facts on File, 1982.

Dahlen, Marsha, and Karen Phillipps. *A Popular Guide to Chinese Vegetables.* New York: Crown Publishers, 1983.

Facciola, Stephen. *Cornucopia: A Sourcebook of Edible Plants.* California: Kampong Publications, 1990.

Larkcom, Joy. *Oriental Vegetables.* Tokyo: Kodansha International, 1991.

Lin, Florence. *Chinese Vegetarian Cookbook.* Hawthorn Books, 1976.

McDermott, Nancie. *Real Thai.* San Francisco: Chronicle Books, 1992.

Nix, Janeth Johnson. *Adventures in Oriental Cooking.* San Francisco: Ortho Books, 1976.

Passmore, Jacki. *The Eclopedia of Asian Food and Cooking.* New York: Hearst Books, 1991.

Toussant-Samat, Maquelonne. *History of Food.* London: Blackwell Publishers, 1987.

Index

(Page numbers in *italic* refer to illustrations.)

Designed by Jim Wageman

Typefaces in this book are Hiroshige,
designed by Cynthia Hollandsworth,
and Spring, designed by Garrett Boge

The type was set and layouts were
created by Laura Lindgren, New York

Printed and bound by
Grafiche Milani, Milan, Italy